Jump Into Janitorial

How to build a cleaning business netting over six figures a year.

By

Ron Piscatelli

authorHOUSE

1663 LIBERTY DRIVE, SUITE 200
BLOOMINGTON, INDIANA 47403
(800) 839-8640
www.authorhouse.com

This book is a work of non-fiction. Names of people and places have been changed to protect their privacy.

First published by AuthorHouse 07/06/04

ISBN: 1-4184-4491-X (e)
ISBN: 1-4184-4490-1 (sc)
ISBN: 1-4184-4492-8 (dj)

Printed in the United States of America
Bloomington, Indiana

This book is printed on acid-free paper.

Acknowledgments

First and foremost, I thank my wife Ellen who has had to put up with me for over thirty years. She deserves all the credit. Thanks to my daughter Pia who typed this book for me and my other daughter Alex who encouraged me every day with her reminders of "Dad, did you get the book done yet?" Lastly, thanks to my dog Patch, who slept the whole time while I worked on this book.

Table of Contents

Preface

I decided to write this book to serve the janitorial industry. I have looked for a book over the years to help me build a business in cleaning. There are only books on how to clean, not on a plan of attack. Finally, a plan is here!

Ron Piscatelli

San Diego, California

Introduction

The janitorial-cleaning industry offers a great way for anyone to go into business for themselves with very little up front money. You can start part time, from home with no more than a sponge, broom, mop and a vacuum as tools. This book is about how to build a business making $100,000.00 net per year and up.

This book serves those who are self employed in the janitorial business and want to expand their businesses. This serves those people who own a janitorial franchise and want to grow their franchise. This also serves those who want to get into the janitorial business. Mostly, this is my opinion on the commercial maintenance business. There are many ways of doing business that I go over. My focus is on simplicity, simplicity in accounts, tools and in a plan of attack.

In the chapters ahead, I will give you simple ways to build a business that can provide you a comfortable living with a stress free environment. Can being stress free and running a janitorial business be said in the same sentence? Yes! It takes knowing what your goals are. In the beginning chapters, I go over picking an area of cleaning to focus on and the one I recommend. I define my "perfect client profile," then how to market and sell. In the middle chapters, I go over hiring and training. The last chapters go over incentives and putting fun into the business. So, let's get started.

CHAPTER ONE

Decide on a Niche

Decide on a niche

In this chapter, we will be discussing: What type of company do you want to have?

* The many niches of the cleaning industry there are.

* My perfect client profile.

* Comparing the benefits of a large building account to a small janitorial account.

* We will go over a plan to net you a six figure income.

Decide on a niche

Who are you? What type of company do you want to have?

In this first chapter, I want to go over a few different ways that define the janitorial business. There are small and large accounts. There are accounts that require as much as daily service and some that require as little as once per month service. The cleaning itself breaks down to floors or carpets or a combination of both. Then you could break down the industry by the types of accounts available such as supermarkets, office buildings or even restaurants. The one thing they all have in common is that they are of a commercial nature as opposed to a residential nature. There are many more differences in the janitorial industry than I listed above. For over 20 years in the business, I have tried them all. I used to pride myself on the fact that we were always working 24 hours a day, seven days per week. Like the old British Empire saying, *"The sun never sets on British soil,"* so too the cleaning empire I had, never closed. We were always working. Hours of operation is another major decision needed in choosing a niche. The difference now, by my experience, is that I learned that you first figure out what is right for you, then incorporate the aspects of the cleaning industry that fits your perfect client profile. In other words, twenty years ago when I first started, I thought cleaning itself was a niche. If it was dirty, I took the job.

Looking back, I'm glad I got all that experience, because I then chose a niche for myself that provided me a great income, was easy , was a stress free way of life and gave me a lot of free time. I wish when I started out, I could get the advice I am giving in this book, especially in deciding a niche. I could have saved fifteen years of errors. I plan to first list the different niches I have worked in over the past twenty years. Then, I will list the niche I chose and will outline it. I believe that if you focus on one niche,

you will do better than if you do them all.

<u>The many niches of the cleaning industry</u>

* Air Duct Cleaning

* Auto Detailing

* Carpet Dyeing

* Commercial Carpet Cleaning

* Commercial Janitorial

* Construction Clean-up

* Drapery Cleaning

* Flood Repair

* Floor Stripping and Waxing

* High Pressure Washing

* Marble Floor Polishing and Restoration

* Navy Housing Vacants

* Party Serving

* Residential Carpet Cleaning/Upholstery Cleaning

* Residential Maid Service

* Window Washing

* Wood Floor Restoration

* Vacant Move Out

First I decided what was important to me. I wanted my wife home with the kids all day. I wanted to be home all day too. I wanted to work from home, yet not have any worker come to my house. I wanted all day off to enjoy life, yet be able to build my income. This lead me to the type of accounts that I wanted.

My perfect client profile

I decided on easy, small, one or two visits per week, done on Sunday through Friday nights, accounts, cleaned from 6PM to

11PM only. The type accounts that only required tools consisting of a vacuum, broom, feather duster and small mop. My goal was to charge $100.00 per hour of labor and I wanted the accounts clean when I got there. (*I do not like to clean dirty places.*) I also insisted on cleaning for people with whom I had a good rapport and where we had mutual respect for each other. I also love five days per week, large accounts dealing directly with the company hiring us.

Accounts I no longer love

My whole way of thinking came about slowly. I used to love the 100,000 square foot, five days per week office building accounts dealing with property managers. I could net big money, but there was a great deal of involvement in those type accounts. You had about 100 bosses all with different agendas. Office buildings are made up of small companies each paying enormous rents each month. They think and are lead to believe that they will get hand maid service as part of their rent. Sometimes they are at odds with the landlord. On second thought, they are always at odds with the landlord and we are stuck in the middle.

Janitorial companies charge from five cents to fifteen cents per square foot per month for five days per week service. I also charge $150.00 per floor for commons work. A suite that has 1,000 square feet would only pay, (@ 7 cents per square foot), $70. per month. Broken down to only 20 working days a month, (there are more some months), that's only $3.50 per visit that is charged. That's like nothing, yet when added to a large amount of square footage, it does yield a profit. I would calculate about $1,000 net profit per 50,000 square feet. Most janitorial companies fight for these accounts each month and sell their souls to satisfy all those tenants, not to mention the property manager. I found that when you have a property manager that you have rapport with, you can communicate and understand what is needed to be done and can keep these accounts. Unfortunately, property managers, are always coming and going. Buildings are bought and sold. New managers come in and bring their own janitorial companies.

Then, one day, I was looking over my most profitable accounts. I had small accounts that were 500 square feet and needed service only two times per month. They were paying $99.00 a month, for just two visits per month. These accounts took about thirty minutes for one person to clean, because they were small offices, they had a commercial grade low pile carpet and usually only one rest room floor. Places a little larger have a small kitchen floor. I don't always get $100 per hour. I will take $30 per hour if it is convenient, easy, and next to another account that I do. What really amazed me was that because they were next to another account I was doing, I only paid thirty minutes to an hour's pay to a janitor to clean it. On top of everything, those small accounts were cleaned so infrequently, that their own workers had to keep it to a certain cleanliness during the month. I loved these accounts, because I usually dealt directly with the owner or manager and our relationship lasted. There were no hidden agendas. They appreciated my service. I settled on keeping smaller office buildings. Fifty thousand square feet or so was the highest I sought although I would bid on bigger ones when referred, but charged a very high price for the effort. I did not always get these. When I did, I liked making extra money. In a 50,000 square foot building your monthly man hours to clean it would be around 245 hours a month. That would yield $1,000 net per month. Notice the comparison to the small account theory.

50,000 Square Foot Building	Small $99/Month, 2 visits (12 accounts)
1.) 245 man hours a month	1.) 12 man hours a month labor time,(1/2 hour per place to clean& 2 visits per month each). I would pay people one hours pay per place, or 24 visits hours a month
2.) Net profit $1,000 (after labor and taxes) *See breakdown at the end of this chapter	
3.) Deal with 30 tenants, none of whom hired you	2.) $900. net profit per month unless you do the 12 hours work and keep all the $1,200. monthly
4.) Need special buffers, waxes, equipment, etc.	
5.) Always hiring, classified ads costs, interviewing costs, hard to cover, absenteeism,	3.) Deal with 12 owners, all of whom hired you and you have rapport.
6.) Always dealing with some customer issue at the building	4.) Easy work, simple need only vacuum, duster, mop
7.) Having own office location is important because of the volume of interviewing and the storage of equipment. Also a large number of employees.	5.) Very little to cover if janitor calls in sick
	6.) Never hear from a customer
8.) Need a secretary Ie of volume of calls from customer, applicants, people traffic for Interviewing, training, etc.	7.) Could work from your home, no over head
	8.) Voice mail system all that's required
9.) At Christmas time, have Christmas parties to clean, trees to remove and special vacuuming for needles.	9.) Have rapport with owners- and get presents & thanks.

I could go on and on. As you can see, I fell in love with small, easy, money making accounts. Everyone is happy. The customer feels like they are getting a bargain. Ninety dollars seems like nothing for service. They get a top notch professional company. Labor is easy to get, because the jobs are easy. The janitors benefit. I will go over getting labor in a later chapter. You benefit because you could make over $9,000 net a month with only 108 hours of labor a month needed. That's with paying someone else to do the work and paying their taxes and insurances. If you did the work yourself, you would make more. Twenty seven or so hours a week work is not that much. Plus, with all these small accounts, you won't get hurt if one cancels. When a very large account cancels, you feel the monetary difference plus you have labor to re-assign. Let me say, I loved doing larger buildings. It was the constant change of the property managers that I did not like. Once my boss left as the property manager, it was hit or miss if I would have rapport with the new boss. After all the time it takes to meet each tenant and learn how to satisfy each one, a new boss may have their own cleaning company to use instead of us. Large buildings that are occupied by a single owner that needed five days per week service are my ultimate favorite account.

The accounts you get will all vary in price, labor and the frequency of service. The bottom line is that you could do them between 6 PM and 11PM on any day or after as you choose. The other aspect is keeping your overhead low by doing places that take very little specialized equipment. This is the type niche I will be talking about throughout the book. Recruiting of labor and all marketing will be highly effective when you are focused. Later on, you can add related services as an add on, but the more focused on a segment of the market and you will come up with ways to accomplish your goals much quicker. Again, this niche served my needs. I wanted to enjoy life, have free time, be home with my family and have that great feeling of independence by not being financially dependent to any one account. Every niche of the industry I have listed in this chapter is just as good as any other. I just picked one to keep things simple and picked a niche to become great in. This book is about the easy janitorial niche. Just figure what's important to you.

You don't have to stop at $9,000 per month net. This is the first step to accomplishing your goals.

(For more info on setting goals, writing a business plan, and an organization chart, read *Coffee Break Wisdom on Building a Successful Business*. For a free copy of a business plan & mission statement outline, Go to www.CoffeeBreakWisdom.com).

The following breakdown explains the labor costs from the above chart.

A "50,000" square foot building breakdown

*50,000 square feet @ 6.5 cents per foot = $3,250 gross plus $500 to cover 3 floors of commons. The total charged per month comes to about $3,750. That building takes 245 man hours to clean per month and @ $8 per hour labor, then after taxes, workers comp and liability insurance = $1,000 monthly net.

Note: Workers comp and liability insurance vary from state to state.

Net income is an approximate amount.

Review of chapter one

In this chapter we discussed:

* The type of company you want to be.

* We talked about all the different aspects of cleaning and how each has a niche of it's own.

* We went over my perfect client profile and how this book is about that niche.

* We compared what it would take to do a larger type account as opposed to a smaller one.

* We compared accounts in a long chart for each point.

* We went over how this plan could net you six figures a year and how to have free time doing it.

Ron Piscatelli

CHAPTER TWO

OVERHEAD

How much overhead do I need

In this chapter, we will be discussing:

*   How much overhead do you need?

*   What is overhead?

*   Do you need an office and a secretary?

How much overhead do I need?

"If you want to make money, stop growing." That was a quote I heard from a bank president in San Diego when I first got into business 20 years ago. I resisted it. I read books such as *"Think and Grow Rich" and "*The *Magic of Thinking Big"* and other books such as those that encouraged growth. How could my banker say to not grow? Now, I know what he meant. He meant grow profits, don't add over-head expenses.

Over-head includes any expense that has to be paid every month whether you make a sale or not. That would be your office, secretary, in house bookkeeper, electricity, telephones, pagers, cell phones, full time labor, management, loans, car/truck/ equipment installment payments. The list could go on and on. This is where all of your profit goes. If you are not frugal, your spending takes away from your profits. That's why I love the niche I recommend in this book. You need very little equipment. Supplies are minimal.

When I was cleaning supermarkets, we had to have the latest equipment like propane burnishers, propane edgers, automatic floor machines, wax laying machines, scrubbing machines, wet vacuums, the small tools like mops, buckets, hand squeegees and large wind movers. Don't forget a mop cleaning service to wash your mop heads.

When you take on large floor accounts, it requires a great deal of equipment and delegating the work takes a great deal of training. The hours of work are in the middle of the night. These type of accounts are easier to get than the easier janitorial accounts I recommend, because not as many companies can do the work in a quality manner. You get a great deal of satisfaction from your results when you do great work. I'm not saying not to invest in this area of the cleaning industry. I'm pointing out how over-head can creep into your budget without you realizing it. When you start your first floor you decide you need a wet vacuum, then a buffer. Then you need a propane and we are off to adding high over-head.

Should you get an office? That's a decision you have to make. All I want to say is that an office is not needed to make money in the janitorial business. When I was growing my business, I thought that I would never attract employees without one. When you decide on the niche you want to pursue, you can decide if an office is necessary. How can you work without an office if you live in an apartment? In the niche that I am recommending, you will need very little labor. I interviewed my potential labor at a coffee shop or at one of the accounts I planned for the new recruit to work. I met in the parking lot after business hours when the account was closed. I used an account's storage room for my supplies and a communication point I had with each janitor. Checks are mailed two times per month directly to the janitor. Usually one or two of your accounts will provide you with a huge storage room for your main supply room. Even if you had to rent a storage room, it is not as expensive as an office.

As for having a secretary, depending on your cleaning niche, you may not need one. With today's technologies, voice mail systems and computers save so much time and labor. Voice mail appears professional. If you are in carpet cleaning or vacant home cleaning, you may want a live person to answer the phones. You need a live person to answer the phones if you use the yellow pages for your advertising. People who use the yellow pages go on to the next ad where someone will answer their questions right away.

Review of chapter two

In this chapter, we discussed:

* What growing means and how to avoid overhead.

* We discussed what overhead is and how it can grow without you realizing it.

* We talked about how much labor to have and ways to cut out overhead.

* We talked about items you really need to conduct a janitorial business.

Ron Piscatelli

Jump notes

CHAPTER THREE

How big do you want your business?

How big a business do you want?

In this chapter, we will be discussing:

*   Your dreams and how they relate to the size of business
    you will want to grow.

*   We will talk about ways to accomplish the amount of
    money you want to make.

*   We will go over what you can do with your free
    time.

How big do you want your business?

The best way to decide the size of the business you want is to first list the items in life that are important to you. No need to think about the costs at this point. Just list what you would like to happen in your life. Let's say you wanted a 20 room mansion in the most expensive area of town with a spectacular view. That would take building a larger business with a greater net income than if your goal was for a 4 bedroom home in the suburbs. Making this list of things you want goes into your whole lifestyle.

(A more in depth study is done in my first book, Coffee Break Wisdom on *Building a Successful Business*. Go to www.CoffeeBreakWisdom.com).

This chapter illustrates a plan to net $100,000 or more in the easiest and quickest way, with as little over head as possible. I focused on easy accounts that took very little equipment.

31

In chapter one, I explained the niche this book will focus on, easy, repeat janitorial accounts requiring simple tools. Their hours of operation close by 11PM. You can get any combination of 5 days per week accounts to once or twice a month. To follow the $100,000 net per year example, the gross monthly income would have to be between $12,000 to $15,000. The larger the account and frequency of the service will determine the hourly rate to charge. The bigger the account, the less you make per hour. That will require a higher gross income to be sure that after you pay labor, taxes, insurances, supplies and other costs, you make at least $8,000 net per month.

When doing the work yourself, you are going to be tempted to offer added services like carpet cleaning. It is very easy to go out and buy a carpet cleaning machine. I say do not do it. Most people start with a portable water extractor type cleaner. When I first went out to clean a carpet, I made $250 on my first job and it only took me an hour to do. Then, the neighbor wanted her house done and I made another $200 right away. It was very intoxicating to get $450 for a couple of hours of work and a couple of hours to set up, take down including driving time. In actual work, I was making over $200 per hour and that was for carpet cleaning only. I knew in the future, I could sell customers upholstery cleaning, teflon protectant and other related sales. The problem came for me when I upgraded to a truck mount. Fifteen years ago the truck cost me $30,000. I needed a full time mechanic, because those machines take pampering. There was maintenance and insurances. The carpet cleaning business is a great business. I did very well in it. How many businesses do you want to be in at the same time? Carpet cleaning is a different business than janitorial. Trying to be good in both at the same time makes you mediocre in both. I would recommend hooking up with a carpet cleaner who is self employed where you can do a 50-50 split. They are out there.

I decided to just focus on easy janitorial accounts. If that's what you focus on, that's what you will eventually get. I was amazed that when I focused on my niche and it grew, I had all day practically free. I had very little activity in my business. When I had 75 employees, I was always dealing with issues, but it was fun at the time. As I got older, my priorities changed and I wanted to enjoy life with my family. Imagine having all day off in the cleaning business yet growing. I get no calls from customers because they are happy and have set schedules. I keep employees. I only hire part timers. They used this job as supplemental income. More on that in the hiring-recruiting chapter. I do market, using a part time telemarketer and go out on select bids so my time involvement is minimal. This is all because I chose my niche and focused on one thing. It took a while to get all of the accounts I wanted to reach my target income, but once I got them started, my time and involvement was minimal.

What can you do with your free time everyday? You could do more marketing and get more business. You could devise ways to invest, buy property, and build your assets. You could write a book. This is my third published book. The point is you can create a janitorial business that can provide you a quality existence, a great income and give you the things you want, not to mention having a great deal of free time.

I want to emphasize that the more days per week that an account takes to clean, the lower the hourly charge per man hour. Some as low as $15.00 per man hour.

Review of Chapter three

In this chapter, we discussed:

* We went over your dreams and how they relate to the size of business you want to have.

* We talked about ways to accomplish the amount of income you want to make.

* We went over what you can do with your free time.

Ron Piscatelli

CHAPTER FOUR

Marketing

Marketing

In this chapter, I will discuss:

*Door to door marketing.

*Network meetings.

*Telemarketing.

*Yellow pages ads.

*Newspaper ads.

*Websites.

*Imprinted products like pens, magnets, pads of paper, etc...

Marketing

I like to think of marketing as I would think of working in my garden. The more seeds I plant, the more plants that grow. In marketing, the idea is similar. You plant your name in the minds of those people who fit your niche. As the needs of those people in your niche surface, your hope is that they give you an opportunity to bid for the account. This is not the time to make a sale. I think this is where salesmen get confused. The minute they meet someone, they talk, talk, talk about the service they are selling, or they focus on instant success.

The first plan then is to have different approaches to marketing and sales. So the focus is to get your name in the hands of people who fit your niche. This book is about the niche I recommend. In my recommended janitorial niche, we have small businesses that close at 6:00 PM. I like accounts that are not that dirty. (Restaurants are very dirty. Convenience stores are dirty. They are open after 11:00 PM. I would not take these accounts.) Let me say here that when I first started in the cleaning business, I took anything I could get. I took a lady's health spa that I got paid $2.50 per hour and worked at three AM. I used this account as a reference to get me more accounts. After I filled up with business, I raised these low paying accounts. Most did not stay with me, but they got me the type of businesses that fit my niche that I really wanted. Plus they gave me experience on how to clean things.

Door to Door

I look for small 500-3,000 square feet accounts that are usually offices of some sort.

#1) Small accounts that use service one time per month. You can make over $50. per hour.

#2) Small accounts that use service two times per month. You can make $50. to $100. per hour.

#3) Small weekly accounts that use service one time per week. You can make $50. to $75. per hour.

These are the accounts I looked for, easy places to clean. This is the goal I set. If I liked a customer, they were next door to another job I was doing, or the job was easy work, I could drop the price.

So if you clean yourself, you would need 100 customers that were bi-weekly and paid $100 a month for the service. That would give you $120,000 per year. That would mean you would have 50 customers to service weekly. It takes one person 30 minutes per location to clean. That would mean working 25 hours a week or 5 hours a day, 5 days a week. You could hire a part time worker for 25 hours a week and work minimally along side. Once you established your accounts, your marketing could be reduced to minimal amounts just to maintain your income. With 100 different accounts, your income is more secure than if you did one $10,000 account per month. You lose that big one and you are broke. Now you have your whole day off to enjoy your life. You could build an even larger business. I will give you ideas for management and organizing as if you do want to build a larger business.

Next, I am going to list a few ways to market. Let me first say this. If you had to market yourself, there is no easier and cheaper way to market then door to door. By doing it yourself, you will know exactly where the account is and the size. You can tell right away if you like the people. This may be the way to start with a small advertising budget. In the example on the previous page, we said it would take one hundred accounts paying $100 per month or any combination of accounts that add up to $10,000 monthly gross that repeat each and every month.. It has been my experience that I could get one account or very good hot prospect every hour I went door to door. My simple, but steady approach could get you all the accounts you need in six months.

You may be thinking that you do not like sales. I would hate sales if I had to make them door to door. I did not go door to door to make sales! I went door to door to market my services. Remember, marketing is not sales. Marketing is planting seeds. You want to sell the notion that when the customer is ready for a new service, to please keep your card and give you a chance to give an estimate, nothing more. I used to go into a location, ask for the owner or manager and just say I wanted to leave a card and that was it. By having that as my focus, (leaving a card), no pressure was put on the prospect. After I gave my card I would ask if they use a service now and if they were happy. If they said yes they were happy, I would say, "I hope your cleaning company wins the lottery and lives happily ever after. Would you please keep my card?" Most would laugh and say yes. I didn't say a word about how good my company was. They do not care at this time

At least one time per hour someone would say they were unhappy, want an estimate in a month or two when their contract was up, or I would get a carpet cleaning job. Something good always happened. Even then, my approach to prospects was to probe with questions and listen for answers. I will get into that more in the selling section.

If every person you saw door to door bought from you, you would love going door to door. Everyone would. It's being told "NO" that make people hate going door to door. Who likes that humiliating feeling of rejection? When people do say no, it has nothing to do with you. Don't take it personally. Everyday we all have priorities that we have to accomplish. We deal with our needs. If what you are selling is not a need at this time, why would someone want to talk with you? That's why when you focus on the point that you are marketing, (not selling), you do get a victory when someone takes your card. Everyone I see takes my card. They could throw it away once I am out of sight. I know I throw many cards away once a salesman leaves my office. I keep the cards of the people who seem professional in their approach of marketing.

I do not want to make it sound like I invented going door to door or that I love it. I would rather be on a beach somewhere than go door to door. When I was in need of new business, this was always a part of the many ways that I marketed. I always wanted ten different ways to market going at the same time. I was also lucky in that I had a good coach/mentor that led me to door to door. That person was my wife, Ellen. When we were just married and worked for other people, we joined an Amway group. One Saturday my wife asked if I wanted to go door to door and sell soap from Amway. I said, yelling, "NO." They (Amway Representatives-distributors) said that if we use the products ourselves and recruit a couple of people a month who do the same, you won't have to market. My wife said, "I know." "I wasn't asking you to go." "Stay home and watch the football game." I said "Okay." About an hour later, she came back with all smiles. I said, "What are you so happy about?" She said, "I met the neighbor across the street and he is a doctor. I met this other neighbor around the corner and he is a lawyer. His wife was friendly. They were a nice couple. I think you would like them. Another neighbor owns their own business." She made it sound so great I asked right then in the middle of the football game, "Would you go out with me right now?" Of course she said yes and I had the same fun as she did meeting people in my neighborhood.

That's the experience I have whenever I go out. No, not everyone is nice. I've learned to focus on what goes well, not on the ones that go bad. This is just one way to market. You could hire someone to do this for you. Everyone associated with my company always markets in their everyday travels. If you are on a bid, pass out a card to the neighbors, at least on each side. When you go to a store, pass a card out at 2 to 5 stores around it. Just be aware of doing it.

Intuitive Marketing

Like in the Star Wars movie when Obywan Canoby told Luke to relax and let the force be with you, Luke shot and destroyed the space station, you too can let go. Let the Force show you the way. The point is relax and allow your intuition to point out potential accounts for you to call. I asked the Universe

(God) to shine on companies that needed my services. Then, as I was driving down a street, a name of a company would appear. I could be stopped at a red light for instance and all of a sudden notice a company sign. I would think "I wonder who is cleaning them?" I then would write down the name and address. Later at my office, I would look up the phone number and call. Some people say I was lucky, but I got a lot of business this way.

Wrong Phone Number

Ever have people call and dialed wrong? Before they hang up I say "It may be fate that you dialed wrong! If you ever need a cleaning company, give us a try." I got two customers this way and I rarely answer phones. I always wondered how many I could get if I answered the phones all day. The idea here is to be alert at all times about your business to market, not sell.

Visualize Before Marketing

Before any activity, I relax and go into a meditation state. Basically I get my brain waves to a slow speed called the "Alpha State." This is like the state you are in when you just wake up in the morning. You are conscious, yet asleep. I picture a scene of where things go as I want them to as if they already happened. I do this before I do my marketing. I do this for sales too. This improves your results. The only limitation is remembering to do it for everything. I always get parking spaces. I never did before I used this technique. I used to be frustrated with taking short flights from San Diego to San Francisco where there were no assigned seats. It was first come first serve. You got a number to board the plane. I always wanted an aisle or window seat and feared being next to someone disgusting. I then decided that I wanted a middle seat. I visualized having interesting and successful people next to me on each side. That's what I got. There was always someone interesting. I made contacts every time. I was almost sorry the flights ended, they went by very quickly.

NOTE: If you purposely insert the image of what you want to happen, your chances will improve that it will happen as you see it in your mind. You are doing it anyway, (visualizing what will happen), without realizing it. You may be seeing or fearing what you don't want to happen. That is the surest way to sabotage your results, of what you want to happen.

Network Meetings

A network meeting is where business people gather on a regular basis to meet other business people and to exchange cards. Your local Chamber of Commerce has monthly meetings.

There are groups like "Le Tip" or "Exchange clubs" that meet and promote each other through referrals. Any type of meeting is networking. At some like a political meeting or your church meeting, you have to do more relationship building before you promote your business. The idea is the same as door to door. Do not sell! You are there to market. You want people to take your card and hold onto it so that when the need arises, they will call you. The best way to get people to take and keep your card is never talk about yourself. Ask the person you meet about his business. Ask a million questions as if you are interested in that person.

In janitorial, if your plan is for larger office buildings, then you can go to network meetings that deal with that niche, BOMA (Building Owners and Managers Association) or the Real Estate Association. There is a meeting for almost any group. I would always come away from a network meeting with a great contact/

prospect. One great lead would represent a great day and I always got at least one. The way I look at things, two out of every ten people you meet will love you. Two out of the every ten people will hate you. Six could go either way depending on how they meet you. For example, if one of your friends introduced you to a friend you might like that person more than if you met them at a football game and they spilled a beer down your back while rooting for the other team.

At network meetings and going door to door, my strategy was to look for those that loved me. When I first went to meetings, without thinking, I always pursued those that I loved or wanted to meet. If you really pay attention to people, they all pursue the ones they want to meet. Sometimes the ones that want to meet us are ignored by us, because we are so self centered and are thinking of ourselves and the people we want to meet. Business is the reason for the meeting and you have to make the most efficient use of your time.

I started making great contacts once I started paying attention to the people who sought me out. I could still give a business card to people I wanted to know, but not as the first priority. The first priority was to make contact with the one or two who wanted to know me. The world is a wonderful place in that someone out there likes someone. Not everyone likes the same people, but it seems like there is a perfect match for everyone. Yes, there are always a couple of people who seem to be overly popular, but most of us are not. Yet, no matter how unpopular you may be, there are still one or two at a meeting that will click with you. <u>Notice them!</u> If you pursue the ones you like first, the ones that like you might leave the meeting, or may just not seek you out again. These are important contacts that cultivated on a regular basis will make all the difference over a period of time.

Ron Piscatelli

The idea is to create contacts that will either use you now, use you in the future and/or refer you to someone they know. At the Le Tip type network meetings, you are with the same 20-30 people every week. You can create 20 salespeople out there looking for accounts. First, tell others what you are looking for. I would say, "I do janitorial services for professional offices that close by 11PM at night. People would know what I do. I would then say, if you know of or meet any owners of small business that have offices, please think of me. In two sentences I could explain what I want. My goal was one sale a month from this program. In these type of network meetings, no one cares about you. They care about themselves. If you want people to think of you when they are out in the world, get them business first. Go out of your way to pay attention to the professions of those other people in your group. Find them business referrals. They will be so grateful that you and your business will be on their minds. You will get a steady stream of referrals. When you give to others, they give back to you.

In many organizations, the best way to market yourself without appearing self serving is to take on responsibilities of the group. Take on new membership duties. This way you get to meet the new people. I liked to be on the speakers bureau where I recruited speakers to talk at our meetings. There are many business leaders that would love to give a 15-30 minute talk. I first invited the person by phone and I got to know them a bit. When they came to the meeting, I was their contact and we had a bond as if we knew each other. I got to meet many great contacts worthy of talking at our meeting. Being involved results in many of the top people of the organization to be familiar with you and what you do.

When new members seeking to come to a meeting called, I took the calls about membership. Many times I first met with the potential member for coffee. By the time they went to the meeting, we had a bond and I introduced them around. They had confidence in me and I had credibility. This transferred to my business without me having to sell myself or sell the benefits of my business.

Telemarketing

Calling businesses for new accounts is the best way to get new business. Door to door is the best if you have no money in your marketing budget. Telemarketing if done right can be very effective. The problem with this area is your experience with hiring the right people. If you have no experience, you will make mistakes in hiring people. I have experience in hiring people and I make mistakes from time to time. You have to keep looking for what you want, until you get it.

What do you want? I wanted a telemarketer who could work from home and produce. There are many experienced telemarketers that would love to call from home. I paid very high pay per hour. I loved it when someone wanted $10 to $15 per hour. Of course they had to produce. In a four hour day, I would welcome one great bid, in my niche that needed to switch companies right away. I could get 2-4 leads an hour to just give free estimates. I decided that I was just doing good "PR" work, by going out to just give a free estimate. Then I used my time in the best and most efficient way. I only went on bids that needed a new company to start right away. It may seem like I paid a lot for telemarketing, I did. I maintained my income with this one simple method giving 10 hours a week to the telemarketer. I trusted the telemarketer. One in particular stayed with me over 5 years. I always had good rapport with my telemarketers and they all lasted with my company for years.

Like all marketing, it takes time to learn what you can do with a particular method. With the phone, do it yourself. Learn what results you can get. Then it is easy to know what to expect from someone you hire. If you do call yourself, I would rent from the phone company, a business directory listing businesses by the street. This way you can concentrate on the same area of town. Start with the free yellow pages, then upgrade to a better business directory to make calls from.

I would call the business and say "Hi, my name is ____ and I'm with a janitorial company. Could you tell me who the person is that hires janitorial?" They tell me. I ask if that person is available. When the person gets on the phone I say, "My name is ____ and I'm with a janitorial company. Are you the one who would hire the janitorial service?" If yes, "Are you happy with your service?" If yes, say thank you and hang up. If no, ask if they are on a contract. If yes, when can you call back. If no, ask if you could give a free estimate.

It is really as simple as that. I don't even tell them what company I am from until we set an appointment. They don't care and I don't waste words. I go out where people need me, they are happy to see me and I can sell at ease.

If a decision maker is not in, I ask the secretary if they use a service. I ask if they are happy and ask their advice on how to meet the decision maker if they are unhappy. I just go with the flow. I would hate marketing if I got insulted all day. I would only get insulted if I tried to convince someone why my company was great when they do not need to change their company. So relax and market. I can not say it enough. Just ask questions and get people talking. No one cares what you have to say. If they need your service and they like you, they will ask you.

Yellow Pages

When it comes to janitorial, I am not a believer in the yellow pages. I always placed a small ad in the column with a trade mark logo. I got called from time to time.

When I was in the maid business I usually ran an ad equal to a double business card in size. I got a steady stream of calls, a couple per week.

My belief was that for the money it took to place an ad large enough to get attention, I could use the same money to market where I got a better return. When I got a yellow page lead, that person was comparing me with up to 4 or 5 competitors. I'm not afraid of competition. It is just easier to make sales when you are the only bidder, plus I could choose the type of customer I wanted more efficiently. For your yellow page ad to work, you need to have someone answer the phones or the caller goes on to the next ad. With voice mail systems, potential customers do not leave messages. You will need a secretary to answer phones and this is yet another costly over-head expense. If you are in flood-emergency service, the yellow pages is a must as is the ability to handle the call 24 hours a day.

Newspaper/Display Ads

Display ads in major daily newspapers are very costly. Even when I gave carpet cleaning free, I got better returns elsewhere. I do like inexpensive display ads that are business card size and are in monthly type newspapers that hang around for awhile. Some of these monthly small newspapers go to specific niches of people. Examples: local churches, communities, and business newspapers or local monthly magazines.

In these publications, you may get one good lead per month. Combine a couple of these with other marketing methods and there is always a steady stream of leads coming in. The secret is to be consistent. You have to do it over and over, month after month for your name to be known in that niche.

Website

A website is nothing more than a brochure about you that is accessible to your customers, your potential customers and your local market. It is also a brochure that the whole world could have access to should you choose to sell a related product you can ship. For purposes in describing the plan of this book, I will refer to the website as a local marketing project.

The first thing is keep it simple.

Ideas for web pages and your site

* What makes your company special?

* About your service.

* Place- web address on all printed materials.

* Endorsements listed for credibility.

* Create a customer mailing list.

* Plan an e-newsletter to your mailing list.

* E-mail communications.

* Let customers request services by email.

(For website design, hosting, consulting and other services, go to

www.CoffeeBreakWisdom.com)

Imprinted products

This is a great way to keep your name in front of customers especially if you have a website. Imprinted products like pens, pads of paper, cups, etc... will bring in traffic when you list your website address.

To conclude, the plan is to get 100 customers that pay at least $100 monthly. The more marketing you do, the quicker you will do this. Once you find a marketing method that gives you a documented predictable amount of quality leads, you can increase that method. For example, if you find you can telemarket one hour a day for a great lead, you could then increase the hours of marketing for a predictable day, four hours equals four leads or appointments that day.

Once you know how to bring in quality leads, you can then concentrate on your sales results to see how many of those leads you need to make a sale. What is a quality lead? My definition is a potential customer that fits the niche I defined earlier and has an immediate need for my service. Also, I must meet with the decision maker. Many people may want free estimates, but I only give them for my niche and when they have a need. I don't undercut someone else. I only go out when it is time to change companies. Being professional and filtering your estimates will free up a lot of wasted time and will improve your sales to estimates ratio.

I would force myself on people if it would work. It doesn't. Bugging people about why your service is great is very annoying and will eliminate you from consideration a few months or years later when they would welcome an estimate from you.

Step one in marketing is to experiment with different marketing methods until you find one that consistently produces the results you seek or a combination of ten methods.

Step two is to filter out leads that are not timely in your niche to give estimates to.

Step three is to organize other qualified leads in your niche in a dated file to contact later when their contract is up.

Review of chapter four

In this chapter, we discussed:

* Door to door marketing.

* Intuitive marketing.

* Visualizing.

* Network meetings.

* Telemarketing.

* Yellow page ads.

* Newspaper ads.

* A website.

* Imprinted products.

* The purpose of marketing.

Ron Piscatelli

Jump notes

Jump notes

CHAPTER FIVE

Sales

Sales

In this chapter, we will be discussing:

* First Impressions.

* Be professional.

* Ask Questions.

* Listen.

* Give it away free.

* Know your business.

Sales

The bottom line in sales is results. Without results, you will be out of business. There are many aspects of the sales process and I will go over many of them.

First Impression

You only have one chance to give a good first impression. It happens in the very first moment you make eye contact. Get in the habit that the first thing you do when you look in another persons eyes is smile. Almost always, they will smile back.

These are my estimates and are not scientific, but two out of every ten people you meet will love you. Two out of every ten will hate you and the six in the middle can go either way. What this means, if you are unprofessional, uncouth, unclean with a beard, two out of ten people needing an estimate, will like you. My belief is that if you put a sign on a dog and it went door to door, it would eventually reach enough numbers that the dog will make two out of ten sales. On the other hand, you could be dressed the most professionally and have the best quality service in the world at the cheapest price. You could have a great personality and you still will run into the two out of ten that hate you. In sales, those two extremes are not where you need to work. It's the six in the middle that you want to win over. You can not make every sale so there is never a reason to hang your head if you are not chosen. When you lose an account you are bidding on, it offers you the opportunity to take stock of your approach. Now, back to that first impression.

I have a story that taught me the meaning of a good first impression. One time I was working at an alarm company installing alarms. I was working with a guy named Frankie, (not his real name), and we were paid by the job, not the hour. If we finished installing quicker, we got paid more. At one job we had to run wires along the ceiling on ladders. It seemed that every five minutes Frankie got paged and went to make a phone call. This annoyed me along with the fact that he was unorganized. He could take a two hour job and turn it into two days of aggravation for me. On one occasion I had an appointment after work and wanted to hurry up so while Frankie was on the phone, I went up and down both ladders, running wires alone to get the job done. I must have done 90% of the job by myself. After the job was done, we were packing the tools when around the corner of the room we were in, we could hear he customer say to our boss, "one of your guys did everything and the other did nothing." I was excited because I anticipated Frankie getting yelled at. My mouth was watering and I was wringing my hands with delight when the customer said, "that Ron guy did nothing, but that Frankie, what a credit to your company." I was in shock. I could not believe what just happened. While Frankie didn't agree that I did everything that day, he did say that my problem was that I walked around with a frown on my face. He said a man once told him that if you walk fast with a smile on your face, people will think you love your job and if you love your job, you must do great work.

Frankie was walking around happy, because I was doing all the work. I was walking around with my shoulders down upset because I was doing all the work. From that moment on, whenever I met someone new, I walked fast and had a smile on my face.

If someone gets a good first impression and they are not the two out of ten that hate you, then you have a great chance to influence eight out of ten people you meet in a positive way.

Once someone gets a good first impression, you practically can do no wrong. If they get a bad first impression, you can never do anything right. Years later I had an experience in cleaning homes. I showed up at a new client's home. I knocked on the door and was greeted by a grouch of an old man. He opened the door and I cheerfully chirped out, "Hi, I'm Ron and I am here to clean your home," showing my ID badge. I was in a uniform and was right on time. He looked at me and yelled while pointing his finger in my face, "I've fired six companies before you and I'm going to follow you around, what do you think about that!"

I had a big smile on my face and said, "Sir, please follow me. And if you find one thing wrong, please tell me. I want to be the best!" He said while still yelling, "Sit down, I want to talk with you!" I said, "Sir, I have to charge you from the minute I arrive. I would rather get right to work and give you good value for your money." He yelled, "I'm paying the bill, now sit down.

Can I make you breakfast?" He went from yelling to making me breakfast.

My good first impression also got me past a big error that day. I was cleaning and I came to the parlor. He had a black grand piano. He wanted me to polish it his way. He had linens he said were twenty years old. He wanted me to spray Endust in the air (not directly on the linen) and catch the moisture of the Endust out of the air by waving the linen around the area I sprayed in the air. He showed me how and said by doing it in this fashion, I would apply the minimum amount of moisture on the linen and thus, the minimum amount of moisture on his piano. He said that my cloth would be like a dry magnet for any dust. He emphasized, "DO NOT GET ANY MOISTURE ON MY PIANO!" It seemed simple enough and I said okay. As I sprayed the Endust in the air, the nozzle got stuck down and came out like a stream, not a light mist. It shot over my cloth and all over his piano. My heart fell into my stomach. I was in a state of shock. I must have reminded him of a Jerry Lewis movie or something, because as I was wiping it off the piano, I looked back to see if he was looking and he was laughing while fixing things on his mantle pretending not to notice.

Later, when I finished, he gave me a tip and a T.V. Had I not made a good first impression, I'm sure he would have kicked me out of the house when that liquid landed on the piano. He used my company for quite a while. With my good first impression, even when I made the worst mistake I could have, he was on my side.

Rules for a good first impression

1.)   Dress as a professional, shirt laundered with light starch military fold for white shirts or work shirts.

2.)   Be clean shaven, clean groomed.

3.)   Be on time.

4.)   Smile.

5.)   Make eye contact.

6.)   Be enthusiastic, peppy and move quickly.

Be a Professional

What is a professional?

A professional knows their business. They know everything it takes to perform in their chosen niche. They act with the highest integrity. They truly believe in their service. They want all parties to win in any transaction.

A true professional will get the job done not only on his good days, but on his bad days. Then, you will never know when he is having a bad day. He will not tell you.

Ask Questions

Once you get to a location to give an estimate, the first thing to do is ask questions. No talking.

Ask if they have a service now. Are they happy? Ask why they want to change companies. Ask what is the important thing they look for in a company. These are starter questions. From their answers you get ideas for more questions to ask. Hold back your desire to answer their questions. Just keep them talking about themselves.

Listening

If people have had a bad experience with a cleaning company, they will want to be heard. By listening and by

83

continually asking more questions, people will get down to the real issues they want solved. Once I know what the <u>real issues</u> are, I note <u>them down on paper,</u> but I still resist answering. I ask them how <u>they think the problem could be solved</u>. The customer usually tells me. Almost always I can agree with their method. I almost never talk about myself. The less I say, the more sales I make.

I usually ask what they are paying. Nine out of ten times they tell me. This gives me a big advantage when giving my estimate. I know the level of quality they are looking for. I come out and ask if they believe I am of quality and can handle the job (If I came in the same budget?). They usually say yes. If they are undecided, I know that they are not ready yet or I didn't get to the root of what bothers them.

After all of my questions and answers, I like to fax them my estimate with my brochure. Then I follow up and ask for the job. I like to be on a pace of about $500 to $1,000 net of new accounts per month. This requires a telemarketer working about 10 hours per week. With a telemarketer, I get two very good leads in 10 hours a week. I get at least one good call back every hour to call when their contract is up sometime in the future. These two qualified estimates in my niche provide me the necessary sales to maintain my customer base and grow. Business customers do come and go due to the business climate and individual industries.

If two qualified appointment estimates per week don't provide you with the amount of sales you want, increase your marketing. Selling, no matter how great you think you are, is still a game of numbers. The more potential clients you meet, the higher number of sales you will make. There is nothing magical about it.

Ron Piscatelli

There was a story of a guy in real estate that made a million dollars a year by going to 100 doors a day. That's a lot of doors by himself. The amazing thing was that he didn't speak English. If he can do it, can you? How bad to you want to make more money?

I went on a bid one time. The client said, "We hate the company we use now." "They break things." "They don't dust." "They don't sweep and they missed powder spilled on floor for three weeks." "I want someone who can clean like me." "Maybe I'm picky." (I kept asking questions to find out all of this). I then asked, "What is the most important thing you are looking for in a janitorial company?" She said "someone thorough because they deal with professional clients that need their displays perfect." I then asked if anything else was important. I kept asking what's important after each answer. She said, "to get things clean." Once clients start repeating answers, I stop asking what's important. I

86

then asked what she was paying. I had planned to give my estimate of $250 per month for once per week service, but held back until I asked her what she was paying. She said she paid $399.

I then asked, "If I had to go up a bit in price, would that stop you from choosing me to get the job?" She said "if a quality company came along, she would be willing to pay higher." At this point I said, "The American Red Cross felt like you do too. The CEO had said we are a company of quality." Then I got back to asking questions. (What I did there is use the customer's words (quality) back for what they wanted. Then, instead of saying, "I'm a company of quality," I let someone else answer for me. One of my happy customers especially a well known local one, like the American Red Cross gives all the credibility I need. If I said I was of quality, it appears like I am bragging or saying things that are self serving. If I let a third party, in this case my customer, say my service was of quality, it is more believable. Just tell the truth using others to talk for you. People can see if you are dishonest. So remember the compliments you receive about every aspect of your service, from your customers. Then, when you are on a sale's call, when a certain aspect comes up, you have a third party comment that will answer for you. My prospects never ask me for references.

Think about it. Imagine not having to give references. That's building trust. I have references, I give people only what is necessary. No more. Many times I never say a word about my company. No one asks. I do send a brochure with the estimate. For credibility, I keep asking questions until I find out the things I need to give them. Then I agree using a third party story that relates what the potential customer is looking for.

Many times salesmen say that they feel uncomfortable asking the client what they are paying now for service. A client can refuse to tell me and it happens. Most times they tell me. In this example, the customer wanted a quality service. I could do the job in less time, but because of the increased price I charged, I added labor for a deeper cleaning. Had I bid the job at $250, the client may not have used me thinking I under bid just to get the account. I gave a "spit shine" type estimate that the customer wanted.

Let's review this sale's call.

I was going to charge $250 monthly.

She said she was paying $399 monthly.

I ask her if I could charge higher and she agreed.

Then I charged less at $375 monthly.

I faxed the bid. She paged me and I got the account. It is amazing when you think about it. I bet I didn't say 100 words during the whole 30 minutes I was there. I did send my brochure that would give the customer confidence that we are a bonafide company. The next day I called the customer and she wanted me to start service as quick as she could cancel her present company. Everyone came out a winner. The customer got a quality service for less than she was paying at the time. The janitor got a higher pay and I made more profit. All this because I asked what the customer was now paying for their service.

I have made mistakes. I had an estimate with a similar type client needing quality and thoroughness. I didn't get what the customer was paying, because she would not tell me. Because I didn't know the costs and because they needed five nights a week of "spit shine type cleaning," I charged higher than I normally do. The client called and said they would use my service. She asked to see my checklists to insure quality. One of my rules is to ask the customers how they would get the job done. Then agree. When she asked me about checklists, that was her way to get the job done. I forgot I was talking to a customer and not one of my janitors. I laughed and said, "I no longer use checklists." "I teach people to clean and either it is clean or it isn't." I forgot to agree with the customer. The customer said she would get back to me and never did. I gave her the impression I wasn't organized. I've lived using checklists for years. I use them, just not for janitors anymore. I use them in the training as you will see in the chapters ahead, when I show janitors how to clean. Then I watch them do it. Then I check up for quality. What I should have said was, "okay, I will get those lists for you. What day do you want to start service? Start at the end of this month or next month?" I would have made $1,000 net monthly from that account had I listened, agreed and talked very little.

Many times when I ask customers questions, I don't agree with their needs. If something is not safe or legal, I won't do it. I also don't take clients that don't fit my niche. It is fun to see people sometimes try to convince me to clean their place once I

tell them I can not do it. Life is too short to work where it is not

a great atmosphere.

Give It Away Free

Another way to get accounts is to clean for free. I have

given cleaning away free especially when I was desperate. When

I needed references this gave me them. If that is what it takes to

get the type of accounts I want, I will do it.

Know Your Business

In any type of sales you do, experience doing the service

or using the product. That is the best way to know the ins and

outs of it. This not only helps you give estimates, it will give you an eye for quality and will build your belief in your company. Belief in your company and service is vital in making sales. You have to believe it before others will believe in you.

In conclusion, let me say I was afraid to sell. When I first started selling, I took my wife on my first sale's call in the alarm business. My wife sat quietly and listened. The customer said to me, "I never saw anyone bring his wife with him." I was thinking, you never met anyone as frightened as me. I was frightened, but I knew I needed to know how to sell. My wife and I went to the library and got sales books. To read faster, I read one and she read the other. Weekly we met to outline the lessons. She would criticize me after a sale's call. I never did anything right and it was usually because I talked instead of listened. From the Godfather movie there was a story about the character Sonny. He was in a meeting with the other crime family bosses and spoke up when he should have listened. After he spoke up, the Godfather said, "Please excuse my son. He is talking when he should be listening." The faster you learn this lesson, the faster you will increase your sales totals. In the next chapter I will give basic sales packages to help you to give cleaning estimates.

Review of chapter five

In this chapter, we discussed:

* First impressions.

* Being a professional.

* Asking questions.

* Listening.

* Giving it away free.

* Knowing your business.

Ron Piscatelli

Jump notes

Be professional
Ask questions
Listen
Dont talk

CHAPTER SIX

Sales Packages

Sales packages

In this chapter, we will be discussing:

* What is a small account?

* Small accounts that are weekly.

* The three types of five day service packages.

* "Premium Maintenance Service."

* "Class "A" Office Service."

* "Surgical Service."

* How to estimate labor.

* A labor estimating chart for five day accounts.

Sales Packages

Having pre-set programs makes it easy for people to choose your service. If you are just starting out, set prices can help you give estimates. (Asking what they are paying helps even more). Looking for accounts that fit the niche discussed in this book would mean smaller type offices that can be cleaned during early evenings. Small office type accounts, based on 500 square feet to about 3,000 square feet, that are done on a regular basis, takes about thirty minutes. As the office gets to the 3,000 square feet size, I pay a janitor an hour's pay. No matter the size, there is a minimum charge I have and that is up to 3,000 square feet. The items that take time to clean are the rest rooms, floors and kitchens. Small offices usually have one or two rest rooms and a kitchen.

Even if you bid every small account at $199 or higher, if you have rapport with the customer, they will either accept this price or ask you to lower it. That means you can lower the price to get the bid. The key of course is building rapport. I never just lower the price. I decided if I want to lower it. I first ask if besides the price, there are any other issues. If they say no, I say, "then you are saying that if I can lower the price $25 (or whatever they want me to lower it, and I can do it), you will go with our service?" If they say yes, I say I can lower it on one condition, "that if you are happy, will you let me use you as a reference?" They are glad to do that on the condition they are pleased with my service. Sometimes I won't lower it if asked because the work is difficult. I usually do lower it a bit for my potential new niche accounts because they are easy to do and easy to please.

I will first give you a sample of a janitorial sales package I gave my new salesmen when they went out to make sales. This is the base price I start from when I give an estimate. Once you establish this base price you will not need sheets to refer to. These prices can be anything you want. Prices are different in New York City (higher living costs) compared to San Diego. I will give you a sheet that lists the amount of hourly labor needed for larger square footage accounts that require 5 day per week service.

Package (Office Janitorial Account)

Based on 500 to 3,000 square feet cleaned one time per week. This takes one man hour a week labor to clean or 4.33 hours a month. Service includes: Vacuuming, dusting, trash removal, lunch room and rest rooms sanitized. If the account has easy carpets, which means no lines show from the vacuum and no floors other than the rest room and a small kitchen floor, they are my favorite accounts in my niche. These are office type locations.

Ron Piscatelli

High traffic locations that get extra dirty like a restaurant will take much more time and are not in my niche, but you can charge much higher then the estimates below.

Initial Cleaning…………………………..$100.00 to $150.00 one time charge

Monthly Charge…………………………………$150.00 to 199.00 monthly repeat charge

(Labor costs @8.hr, including taxes/insurances = $51.00)

Add a second day in a week service………..$199.00 to $299.00 monthly repeat charge

(Labor costs @8.hr, including taxes/insurances = $102.00)

If a location has plush or dark carpets, (blue/green), or has a larger floor to maintain, then consider adding more time to the labor and a higher charge to the customer. If the account is double the size of 3,000 square feet and still gets cleaned one time per week, double the charge. This is only a base to start from.

I have three types of services for five days per week larger accounts. On the next sheet is my service called "The Premium Maintenance Service."

#1. Premium Maintenance Service

Ideal for:

*Office buildings that provide five days per week janitorial services.

*Schools

*Condominium Centers

* Shopping Centers and Common Areas

* Industrial Applications

Service includes:

*Once per week thorough dusting, vacuuming and full top to bottom rest room cleaning.

*On the other four nights, full rest room cleaning including sanitizing the toilet nightly.

*We will also clean as needed, but not limited to vacuuming, carpet sweeping, spot dusting and trash removal.

This gives the customer the best value for their money.

The next service is called the "Class "A" Showcase Service." because these types of customers demand a deeper, more thorough cleaning. The labor per hour goes up as does the costs.

2. Class "A" Showcase Service

Ideal for:

* Medical Centers.

* Class "A" Office Buildings.

* Hospitals.

*Where the need for a thorough dusting, sanitizing, vacuuming and top to bottom rest room cleaning is required every night.

*Lobbies must be "spit shined" every night to make the first impression for guests a great one.

*You can charge more per square foot for this service than the basic "Premium Maintenance Service."

Ron Piscatelli

The highest quality service I provide is the "Surgical and Medical Service." These type of customers demand an even more detailed cleaning than the "Class "A" Service."

#3. Surgical Application Service

Ideal for:

* Surgical Applications.

* Hospitals

* Medical Centers.

* Dust Free Environments.

* For the customer that has the need to take thorough cleaning to it's limits.

* Disinfecting and sanitizing are done every night.

* All areas are buffed out nightly to create the atmosphere that highly polished, highly skilled professionals work here.

On the next page is an example for bidding on larger buildings that require five days per week service. On the pages after that is a chart to calculate labor hours.

In reviewing how to give an estimate of labor on 5 days per week service (see chart in the next pages) the first column describes categories. The second estimates the amount of man hours per square footage per person needed for labor per night, for the "Premium Maintenance Service." As you follow down the second column, you will see the man hours needed per the square footage, compared to the first column of the size of building's square footage. The third column says what those labor hours would be for the "Class A Showcase Service." The fourth for the "Surgical Service." The last column is for monthly extra floor work usually found in medical buildings with monthly man hours listed. Window cleaning is not counted in these estimates.

To give an estimate for a large building needing five days per week service, you would first estimate the size, the type of cleaning they need and if it is medical or professional offices. To get an approximate measurement of square footage, take the length of the room or building and multiply it by the width. Example: A room that is 100 feet by 100 feet would be a room of 10,000 square feet.

For example:

A 10,000 square foot (highlighted on the chart), building, would take 1.34 man hours of labor per day to clean if it was for the basic service which is the "Premium Maintenance Service." Moving along this row to the right note that for the "Surgical Service," the estimated man hours would be 3.34 for the same square footage.

Using the 3.34 man hours a day multiplied by 5 days per week would come to 16.7 man hours of labor per week.

Note: If this is medical, chances are you will have extra floors in the exam rooms to maintain. Add the extra weekly labor hours in the last column of the chart. In this case of 10,000 square feet, that would add two hours a week to the 16.7 hours which comes out to 18.7 man hours a week to clean that building. Take that 18.7 hours and multiply by 4.33 weeks in a month and you have the total monthly man hours to do that building. For this example we would take 18.7 times 4.33 and the monthly hours is 81. Take the 81 hours and paying a janitor $8.00 per hour comes to $648.00 a month for labor. Taxes and insurances vary depending on the state you live in. In California, a safe rule is to plan on 50% of the labor to go to taxes, insurances and supplies which comes to $324.00.

$648.00 for labor

Ron Piscatelli

$324.00 for taxes, insurances & supplies

$972.00

$972.00 are the costs to clean that 10,000 square foot surgical type situation. It will be up to you to decide the profit margin you want to add to that total.

If you have not cleaned this may seem confusing. A reminder, unless you have been cleaning a location, it may be hard to understand this sheet. There is no substitute for experience, but just for the record, I can clean 7500 square feet to 10,000 square feet per hour (which is the labor estimate for the basic service) on five days per week service, even if the square footage is for medical or surgical. I know how long thing's take to clean. That is what experience is. I never give my employees more than 5,000 square feet an hour to clean. I like knowing I can do double that of which I expect from others to get done. This is another reason my janitors stay with me. I pay by the job not the hour. If I allow a janitor to get paid two hours for a job and it only takes him one hour to clean, he is thrilled to get the extra time. These estimates serve as a starting point to bid.

When you are bidding to a property manager, they may want you to bid the job based upon an amount per square foot per month. Always do the exercise we just did by adding up all of the labor needed, then experiment. Bids on five days per week service are between five cents per square foot per month to fifteen cents per square foot per month on buildings over 30,000 square feet. Under 30,000 square feet and I bid by the job not by square foot. Example: 50,000 square feet cleaned five days per week at five cents per square foot, equals a monthly charge of $2,500.00. I would then deduct the estimated amount of labor, (labor estimates on the chart on the next page) and would establish the profit margin. If that amount of net profit is good for you, give the customer that bid. If you demand more net per account then that is your call. You can raise the amount per square foot you charge the customer. When I am desperate, I always bid lower. Hopefully as you keep adding accounts, you add the ones with the most profit, have the least amount of labor, are the quickest payers and you have great rapport with the owner or manager. Then you can get rid of the customers that don't pay well or are a hassle.

5 Days Per Week Service Labor Chart

Square Feet/Hour	Clean 7,500 Square feet In one hour	Clean 5,000 Square feet In one hour	Clean 3,000 Square feet In one hour	Extra
Carpets Colors:	Commercial Tweeds, Grey, tan	Commercial Pile, Green, Blue Maroon	Shag, Plush Green, Blue Maroon	
Floors	No wax/Min Wax e.g. Kitchenette Small lobby	Tenant Floors e.g. Medical Exam rooms	Tenant Floors e.g. Medical Exam room	

Activity (people per SQ FT	Normal- 1 Person per 100 SQ FT	More than 1 Per 100 SQ FT 2-3 People	Restaurant Beauty Salon Heavily Trafficked	
Cost Expectat-ions	Easy	Semi-White Glove	White Glove	Xtra Floor Hours add per Week floors-wax
	Premium Maintenance 1x wk heavy clean 4x wk maintain	Class "A" Showcase	Surgical Application service	Exam room Floors carpeted Commons

5,000	.67	1.0	1.67	1
10,000	**1.34**	**2.0**	**3.34**	**2**
15,000	2.00	3.0	5.00	3
20,000	2.67	4.0	6.67	4
25,000	3.34	5.0	8.34	5
30,000	4.00	6.0	10.00	
35,000	4.67	7.0	11.67	
40,000	5.34	8.0	13.34	
45,000	6.0	9.0	15.00	
50,000	6.7	10.0	16.67	10
55,000	7.34	11.0	18.34	
60,000	8.0	12.0	20.0	
65,000	8.67	13.0	21.67	
70,000	9.34	14.0	23.34	
75,000	10.0	15.0	25.0	15
80,000	10.67	16.0	26.67	
85,000	11.34	17.0	28.34	
90,000	12.0	18.0	30.0	
95,000	12.67	19.0	31.67	
100,000	13.34	20.0	33.34	20

Review:

Column one: Amount of square feet to clean per day.

Column two: Man hours per day to clean the Premium Service.

Column three: Man hours per day to clean the Class "A" Service.

Column four: Man hours per day to clean the Surgical Service.

Column five: Extra hours to add weekly for floor care.

Note: To be competitive, most labor estimates I gave were in the second column for the Premium Service. The other options were there to give customers a better understanding of the value they can expect.

Review of chapter seven

In this chapter, we discussed:

* What a small account is.

* Small accounts that are weekly.

* The three types of five day service packages.

* "Premium Maintenance Service."

* "Class "A" Office Service."

* Surgical Service."

* How to estimate labor.

* A labor estimating chart for five day accounts.

Ron Piscatelli

Jump notes

CHAPTER SEVEN

Hiring & Recruiting

Hiring and Recruiting

In this chapter, we will discuss:

* What to look for in a janitor.

* Who would clean?

* Defining a niche for janitorial workers.

* Don't be desperate.

* The benefits of cleaning.

* How to screen applicants.

* Good help is easy to find.

Biggest mistake in hiring

When I got in the cleaning business, even though I cleaned myself, I thought that to find labor, I would look for people down and out. Who else would clean? That will be the biggest mistake you make. There are professional people who will clean. The next biggest mistake is working with family. Family members sometimes take advantage because of familiarity.

In the hiring process, I wanted to cut down on turn over. That changed after I had started hiring professional people. I hired professional people to work full time. Professional people will work full time on a temporary basis until they find something else, resulting in too much turnover. However, there are many professional people who are working now and need just a little more money a month. This is ideal!

Ron Piscatelli

There is a great niche of professional workers available for the right program. By the right program I mean, part time work that doesn't take up your whole weekend or include late nights such as a security guard, retail help or fast food worker. Who could maintain a part time job with that type of commitment? Giving part time workers 5-15 hours a week for early evening cleaning is the perfect match to keep professionals for a long time.

With small accounts as I recommend, professional part time janitors, working in their own neighborhoods, will stay with you for years. Even if I had a larger building to maintain, I would split the duties into time periods. At a building that took four man hours a night to clean, I would assign two people a night's work of only two hours a night each. This small work shift made the worker happy, because they could clean at a convenient time and work just enough to make a few dollars. I gave some workers permission to clean at 6 PM right after they left their day job.

Some people like to work, get it done and go home. Other people wanted to have dinner with their families and then go out around 7-8 PM to do their two hour cleaning job. As long as it gets done by eleven PM, everyone is happy. Another great benefit of having two, two hour shifts instead of one shift of four hours, was that if you needed a substitute, the other person would cover.

Hiring family members has never worked for me. If you do, I recommend writing out each job description including goals and responsibilities.

(Organizational chart and job description forms are in the book "Coffee Break Wisdom on Building a Successful Business" at: www.CoffeeBreakWisdom.com)

Another mistake is hiring when you are desperate. It's like the rule when food shopping. "Don't shop when you are hungry."

Ron Piscatelli

The same is true in hiring. Of course you hire when you need someone. Just hold out for what you are looking for. Don't hire anyone! Before I get into screening people, I want to tell a story of an assistant manager in our carpet cleaning division.

One of my assistant managers, who cleaned carpets, let's call him Keith, needed an assistant on his crew. We suddenly got a back log of jobs to get done and ran a help wanted ad. Keith was interviewing and paged me as if it was an emergency. When I called into the office he said with excitement and urgency, that he found the perfect worker. He begged me to rush to the office and approve his choice.

I got to the office and was coming to Keith's office. I could see Keith, but not the applicant who was blocked by the door going into the office. Keith's eyes were big and he was pointing (as not to be seen by the applicant) at the applicant with his head shaking up and down in a yes gesture as if to say, this is the one, the greatest carpet cleaning applicant in the world.

As I entered the room I saw a very over-weight man leaning over filling out his application. As he was leaning over, I could see the crack of his rear end and his lower back. My first thought was, "this guy must have the credentials of a saint to over come what I was seeing before me in his appearance." It didn't stop there. He was dressed in a very shabby way. His clothes didn't fit. He had very greasy hair. As I walked into the room Keith spoke up and said to the applicant, "this is Ron, the owner of the company." He looked at me while turning, like Quasimodo the hunchback of Notre Dame, might turn and look. He turned like he had a stiff neck. As our eyes met, wait, our eyes never met. His eyes went off in two different directions. I asked the applicant if he had carpet cleaning experience. He had none. I asked his job experience, and he had odd jobs here and there. He didn't even have a car for transportation. The person was not hired. Believe it or not, this is how most people hire in our industry when they start. They act totally desperate as if the only people who will clean are transients, criminals or immigrants.

When I picked my niche worker, I picked a professional with a need of easy part time work. My cleaning jobs are easy and I give short part time hours in a flexible time frame. As I do in sales, I listen to the needs of the person I am interviewing. If they have had a full time job for three years and are looking for part time work to either clear debts, pay for a car or something extra, this is someone I look to hire. If I have a route of ten hours a week in the north side of town, I look for a person that lives or works in that area. I'm a match maker. I match the perfect part time job with the perfect professional person looking for an easy part time job. Usually, people who have worked somewhere for three years are dependable, honest and reliable. They have stayed with their full time job and odds are, will stay with my company for a long time.

I used to point out to the applicant that there are so many benefits to part time janitorial as opposed to any other part time position. You are alone when you work so it can be like meditation. When I am cleaning I always visualize in my mind giving speeches at seminars and teaching. The act of cleaning became a trigger to think positive thoughts. I've noticed people who are in such a hurry that they visualize frustrations. I recommend using the time as a special thinking time. For each hour of steady moving, you are doing a low impact aerobic and are burning 200 calories. These are benefits beyond the money. I have had employees who stayed with me for years. When employees stay, customers stay. When I run my help wanted ads I am already trying to screen. I would write in an ad, "part time janitorial, San Diego area, 5-10 hours, must have car, a great second job and phone number, 619-294-7865."

When I interview I look for people in my niche. In the personal interview for the ones that pass the phone interview, I start by judging if someone is on time. If not, I move on. They don't want the job bad enough to take the appointment seriously. If you don't have an office of your own, you can (and I have), met at a coffee shop or in the parking lot of the customer they are to clean, on their night to be cleaned, (I never interviewed inside the customer's place of business, only in the parking lot).

Next, I ask questions about where they work, their experience and learn as much as I can about them. I do not talk until I know I am hiring them or if I am not going to hire them. If not, I say what the job is briefly and tell them I will call if they got the job in the next day or two. The ones I want to hire, I tell about the job and I will get back to them after I call three references. I am not rude to the ones I do not use. I treat everyone with respect. I feel for those out of work. I look for professionals where their situation fits with my needs. I don't care if a person is black, white, gay, straight, man, woman, Catholic, or Jew. I only care about professionals that get the job done. Matching people to jobs increases the odds that you will make a hire that lasts.

In hiring and recruiting nothing takes the place of your experience in knowing the work force available. As you hire more and more, you will sharpen your definition of a professional. I have had many masters degree holders that have worked for me part time. You can recruit those that you are comfortable talking to. I just want to point out that "good help is out there to find." Don't listen to those who say "good help is hard to find." Good help is easy to find when the situation benefits everyone. Everyone wins. The customer wins with good, honest, dependable service. The janitor's hours are easy, part time supplemental hours and I

Ron Piscatelli

make a profit every month with minimal effort once a janitor is

set at the location. My motto is, ***"Good help is easy to find."***

> * This could be an area to hire a coach.
>
> Coaching is available. Go to: www.JumpIntoJanitorial.com

Review of chapter seven

In this chapter, we discussed:

* What to look for in a janitor.

* Who would clean?

* Defining a niche for janitorial workers.

* When hiring, don't be desperate.

* The benefits of cleaning.

* How to screen applicants.

* Good help is easy to find.

Ron Piscatelli

CHAPTER EIGHT

Organizing

Organizing

In this chapter, we will discuss:

* Knowing your goals.

* When to set goals.

* When to work on them.

* Writing in a journal.

* Ask and you shall receive.

* Having free time all day long.

* How to be an idea receptor.

* Priority lists of things to do.

* Total Quality Management and ISO 9001

* Having a consistent service.

* How to write a procedure.

* Keeping graphs and charts.

Being Organized

For me, being organized begins with knowing my niche, knowing my values, knowing my short term goals, knowing my long term goals and then following a plan. (If you need to organize these items, I recommend my other book, *Coffee Break Wisdom, On Starting A Successful Business*, www.CoffeeBreakWisdom.com. This book is geared towards a goal of netting six figures and up).

To be organized, I get my goals written down during the last week of December. I review those goals the last week of August. Those are two perfect times to do this as there is a feeling of a new beginning, because of the New Year and September, the start of a new school year. The last weekend of the month, I review my goals for the month and write out my goals for the coming month. Each weekend I write out my goals for the week.

Each morning I write out my goals for the day. I constantly keep a list of my priorities that I need to do. I write all this down so I won't forget. I also like to keep my mind blank, free from thinking of things to do. I get myself into the habit of waking up by 5 AM every morning including weekends. I wake up automatically. There is something special about being awake before the masses. I have coffee and write in a journal.

This journal keeps track of the issues I am dealing with at the moment. I use it as my crying towel. If I have a problem, I can write it down. I have moments when I'm frustrated and feel like giving up. I get issues off my chest that I would love to tell someone else in person, but I need someone with the skills of Christ, Buddha and Confucius combined, to listen, let me exhaust myself and then have wisdom, wit and ability to say just the right group of words that would give me an "aha" type of experience. I doubt that friend is out there.

The next best thing is talking to yourself. By writing to myself, I am able to place most issues in perspective. As I write in my journal, I keep a paper next to me and as things pop in my mind of what I need to accomplish that day, I write them on that paper. Just writing them puts all I have to do in perspective. It is usually not as much as I imagined before I wrote everything down. Then the most important thing is that on issues I have no answers, I have the ability to at least come up with the right question to ask, so I can solicit answers from others. All of this allows me to keep all issues, goals and things to do in proper perspective. That gives me peace of mind and I'm confident by being mentally organized.

We have all heard of ask and you shall receive. The problem is either not asking, or asking in the wrong manner. Let's say I have a problem, I ask, "how can I get "whatever" and who could I call that might have an answer?" My answer may not come that moment, but it always comes. That was an effective way to ask a question. A non-effective way is to ask, why can't I get "whatever?" Those negative questions solicit answers that affirm the problem. In a sales question, don't ask, "Why can't I make sales?" Ask, "What do I need to do to bring in $10,000 of new business this month?" Who could help give me the answer to building up my sales skills?" In other words, whether in sales, cleaning, accounting or whatever, ask effective questions that give you answers to achieve that which you desire. By the end of my hour with myself writing, I have my list of things to do today. I number them in order of their priority.

I love having a free mind all day. My mind is always getting ideas all day long. I have to keep paper near me at all times to write every idea down no matter how silly. This is the basis of how I organize my day. I am following a list of what I have to get done and I have them numbered in their order of priority. Some days, it feels like I get nothing done, because I have so much free time. I feel like I could do so much more. Then I look at my daily list of things to do, and just about everything is done. If I look at my lists and something isn't done, I make sure I have at least made progress. Then I address why the hold up on my goals?

I see sharp people in business that make money, but are consumed by their responsibilities. They always seem busy, running here or there, always behind, always getting calls on their cell phone. They seem stressed. I have all day off and run a service business. No one ever pages me, no customers or any people. Why? Because everyone is happy. My staff never sees me. They are mature and do a great job. My customers are happy. You never hear from happy customers. I may go on one or two sales appointments during the week. That's all I need to grow and to maintain accounts. Accounts can cancel even if you are a great company because of a million reasons. Other than when I need a new janitor, I have the days off to exercise, read, walk, or meet with people. I spend an afternoon each week, with each of my children, one afternoon per week I go to a movie, I walk each day with my wife going around a lake for 45 minutes. I write books each day. This is my third book in a series of about 20 more to come. I am also an artist and I find time to paint about four paintings a year. (I have no room left on my walls). I meditate each day and visualize my goals as if they are already happening. I work in my yard (close to an acre) and have flowers everywhere. I work on my flowers every other day. The point I am trying to make is I do all of this every day. I have so much free time. I have organized myself to the point where I am free of mind, or rather, my mind is free so it can be an idea receptor. I'm not special. I developed my mind to receive ideas by being

147

organized and asking questions in effective ways. If you work at it, you can do anything you want. After having your goals, your values, your plans and things to do listed, the next step is to list your things to do in order of their priority.

To be organized, I would place on three pieces of paper, all my responsibilities in categories numbered #one, # two or # three. The # ones needed to be done today. The # twos needed to be done in the next couple of days. The # threes needed to be done a week or more.

On my list of number one duties, I list, in the order of their importance, all I have to do. I do this as I write in my journal in the morning. As I was writing, I was making lists. I review my # two and # three duties. Some items become # ones and need immediate attention. I plan how my day will go by placing set appointments on my today's list and working my duties around them.

There is another area that could have you running errands all day. That is buying cleaning supplies. In organizing your cleaning supplies, you need to stock what you need. I keep a marked slot on a shelf for everything. (Keep a fail safe number taped on that marking with a number.) When I or anyone took a roll of paper towels and my fail safe number was 10, then when the tenth was taken, a re-order was issued. Knowing what I used, I was able to negotiate great prices. I also used the same supplies and kept it to a minimum of variety.

For example, I used Sanitaire commercial vacuums. I only had to stock one type of belt. Keep it simple to be organized. This method is also great when keeping track of the customers rest room supplies. If they run out of toilet paper, they will blame you and hate you for that. More about this in the chapter on "The Three Biggest Sins."

Another way to organize is with the "Total Quality Management System," by E. Deming. This is the basic (the same) way to become ISO 9001 certified. I could (and will) write a book just on this subject, but for now, I want to touch base on it. You may want to make it your five year goal to know this subject. This is your first lesson. This lesson is a brief overview.

To keep it simple on how it pertains to janitorial, your goal should be to provide a consistent service that meets and exceeds the customer's expectations. Should your service move off of that expectation, you want to be the first to know, not the last. By being the first to know, you can get it back on track. If the customer never knew you went off track, did you go off track? If we were a football team and I fumbled and you, my teammate recovered the fumble, was it a fumble? Obviously no, if you catch the error before the customer sees it, it is not a complaint.

Another way to look at it is like when you drive a car. You have gauges. Your gas gauge let's you know when you are on "E" for empty. You are the first to know. If you do not pay attention, you will be stuck on the side of the road, out of gas. It is the same with business. If you don't pay attention to the customers expectations and the quality of your service slips, you could lose the account. Using this management system is like having a gas gauge that tells you your service quality is getting low and it is time to fill up with super service again.

The next question is, how do you keep your service consistent? Besides retaining labor, the best way is to document the procedure of every task. You may be thinking that you hate writing and how will you ever write down in detail, how to do things. All I can say to that is "do you want to have a free mind all day and the time to enjoy it?" As a small company making

$100,000 net, you won't need to write as many as you think. Start with where you have a problem.

I discovered how to write each procedure when I worked for a boss one time that yelled at everyone for anything. To avoid being yelled at, when I was given a task, I wrote out how to do it and gave it to the owner to verify. He corrected it and I never got yelled at about that task again. I did this because I hated being yelled at. I wrote one for every task I was assigned. That is how to begin, one at a time. Before long, you will be done.

Write a procedure where it seems you are having the most confusion at the time. Keep it in a binder. Eventually, all of them will be done. You do not have to write it perfectly the first time. Just write a couple of lines, you can always add to the list as you go along.

Let's say our task is to make coffee, (this is important to do). Right now list the steps for making coffee.

1.)

2.)

3.)

4.)

5.)

6.)

7.)

8.)

our example:

Step #

1.)   Measure 8 cups of water and place in machine

2.)   Coffee Filter

3.)   8 measured scoops (not a spoon)

4.)   Turn on

5.)   Pour

This is a basic list to make coffee. This is all you have to do and place it in a binder for storage. If the coffee always tastes great no matter who makes it, then this is an effective procedure or process. If you get complaints that the coffee is too strong, you could go to this process and change 8 scoops to 7 or 6. You change until you find the right formula to have consistent coffee. If the taste varies, maybe add a step after step 3 that says, "only buy a certain blend." The idea is to always make changes until everyone who makes coffee makes it the same. Thus consistency!

Every procedure from rest room cleaning, to dusting, to vacuuming, should be written so your staff can do the same job in the same manner consistently. When you give a quality service that is consistent, you will keep accounts. This is not complicated, it's logical. It does take an effort, but no one is upset anymore about procedures, because everyone participates in making the procedure perfect.

As you build your knowledge of this process, you can keep statistics. For example, if you get complaints, keep a list. Then, like a spread sheet, you make a list of each different complaint you got. At the end of the month total the categories.

For example:

Missed mirror in rest room, five complaints in month.

A janitor did not show, one time.

A customer complained that something missed dusting, one time.

From that list, the first process to write (or if it is already written, edit), is the one on how to wash a mirror because it had the most complaints. Or perhaps the procedure on "how to clean a rest room so not to miss a mirror." Maybe the process to write is "how to train someone on the process on how to clean a rest room." The point is that you can pinpoint the problem and correct it. Plus, you will be working on the one that needs the most urgent attention.

Later on, after your processes are written, you can use graphs and charts. They will let you know how you are doing in every area of your business. You will be in step with the pulse of your organization. More importantly, this system gets everyone involved and the potential for profit sharing beyond just being organized, is incredible. When you keep tracking your accounts in this manner, you will be the first to notice problems as with the case of that gas gauge in the car. When your indicator tells you that you need gas, you have to take action. You still have to act. In business, if you ignore your indicator of a customer in trouble or some other item, you will lose workers and accounts like someone who ignores the gas gauge and runs out of gas.

When I get ideas during the day, I write them on separate pieces of paper. That way when I get to my home office, I place them in hanging files pertaining to that project. When that project is being focused on, I will have a huge number of ideas to start with.

This is my basic philosophy that I follow to organize my day. My results have been great. If you knew the people who know me, they would say, that I was always free, any time of the day to meet. Most people wonder if I ever work. I don't blame them. I wonder if I ever work. It helps that anything I do during the day does not seem like work because when you work for yourself, everything you do benefits you and your family.

Review of chapter eight

In this chapter, we discussed:

* Knowing your goals.

* When to set goals.

* When to work on them.

* Writing in a journal.

* Ask and you shall receive.

* Having free time all day long.

* How to be an idea receptor.

* Priority to do lists.

* Total Quality Management and ISO 9001

* Having a consistent service.

* How to write a procedure.

* Keeping graphs and charts.

Ron Piscatelli

Jump notes

CHAPTER NINE

Training

Training

In this chapter, we will discuss:

* Giving new people an orientation.

* How to train cleaning a rest room.

* How to know they know.

* What to do with a slow and thorough trainee.

* The way you start out a new person is the way they will always be.

* Set a good first impression.

* Vertical versus a horizontal world.

* How a professional acts.

Training

Orientation:

I like giving everyone an introduction as to what will happen when they work here. When I was maintaining over 75 employees, I usually had to have an orientation twice per month for 2 to 4 applicants to keep one or two janitors per month. When I used the approach in this book, I stopped the orientation, because I need very few new janitors. After I interview, when I know I am hiring the person, I give the first part. I go over compensation, pay days, raises, expectations, schedules, taking days off, and any other office procedure question type issues. I give the next part of the orientation when I train the janitor at the work locations. I hire them for one night as a trial period. On the first night, I take 30 minutes and go over the rest room cleaning procedure. I show

how to do the rest room and let them watch me. Then I watch as the person cleans one. I usually encourage and direct. I let them clean one on their own and I thoroughly check while they watch. I train until I know that they know how to do the job. "There are no poor students, only poor teachers."

Now, with that said, there is a very important thing to realize. Not everyone may want to work a second job. They said many of the right things, but wanting a second job and doing it are two different things. Sometimes you might have to move on. The person was on a one night trial. Many times they tell me cleaning is not what they wanted after all. Many times they don't tell me but continue cleaning.

It is important to recognize how to proceed. In the book "The Art Of War" by San Tzu who was an ancient Chinese warrior, wrote about a general in a professional army who had a reputation as a great disciplinarian with great success. A local

Warlord asked this general to teach discipline to his army and wanted to know how he did it. The general had the Warlord assemble his harem in the courtyard. The general took the two favorite women of the Warlord and brought them up front. He said to them, "When I say turn to the left, turn to the left. When I say turn to the right, turn to the right." The two women said that they understood his instructions. Then the general asked the women to turn to the right. The women laughed. The Warlord was concerned this test failed. The general said you can't be sure people know what you want by just telling. You must tell and show. The women were then told and shown. Then the general again in front of everyone asked the women to turn to the right. The women laughed again. This time the general pulled out his sword and killed the two women. He then called up two new volunteers. The general showed the women what to do, then had them do it. Now the general said, "turn to the right." This time the whole harem turned to the right instantly in unison.

As a person training someone, you have got to recognize when someone does not do what you know they know how to do. If so, now is the time to let them go and move on. Work only with professionals who don't consistently have the need for you to repeat the same instructions over and over.

Another lesson I have learned on that first night trial period, is if a new trainee is slow and thorough. If they are, they will speed up as they gain confidence in their cleaning. If a person is fast and not thorough, I'm not sure you could ever train them to have a good eye for dirt. Small areas of build up appear that cause customers to cancel us, such as corners, high cobwebs, tops of pictures and finger prints on wall plates. I don't keep fast people who do not notice dirt.

Fast is not the problem. I'm faster than anyone I know, but I have developed an eye for detail and my work is stupendous! I was slow and thorough at first.

The way you train your new employee the first night is the way they will clean in the future. That's why I only let people clean a rest room on their first night and I first have them watch me. I am willing to crawl on my knees if I have to, to get things clean. Your employees will do as you do. I make a point to crawl on my knees, (whether something needs cleaning or not), to set an example. The second night I teach them a small commercial kitchen in an office suite. The next night I teach the office cleaning routine (dust, vacuum, trash, etc.). This book is not about how to clean items. Cleaning procedures and how to clean things will be available in future reports. (To be kept notified, go to: www.JumpIntoJanitorial.com).

Another way to look at the way you first set the example of cleaning, is when you have a water hose on and it flows down your driveway and out of your yard. It finds the path of least resistance on it's search for the ocean and creates a path even on your driveway. If I kept the water on for a thousand years, perhaps a groove in the ground the size of the Grand Canyon would develop. It would be difficult for the water not to follow this path once the groove develops. This is the same when you train all of your people in the exact same fashion. They will follow that path not knowing any other path. They will do it the same way every time. The more you teach it the same way over and over, like the river in the Grand Canyon, your people will stay on course. Your service will be of quality and consistency. Those grooves keep your employees from straying. Do not fool yourself and think that you can tell a new janitor to dust and they will know what dusting is and where to find it.

I like to use titles to remind trainees to remember certain things. For example, a janitor cleaning in front of a customer for the first time, should give a good first impression. Remember the sales chapter when I gave the reason for a good first impression? A good first impression is important everywhere. To do that besides being in a uniform with your ID badge showing, is to have them see you enthusiastically on your knees cleaning under something or along an edge, even if it doesn't need it. I try to angle my rear end up in the face of the customer. I titled this "flash the moon." I give them the impression I am thorough, happy, enthusiastic and I'm willing to get dirty to get the job done right. I never have to do this again. They love me, my company, and never notice a mistake when I do make one.

There is another story of why a first impression is important and how the mechanics of the mind work. Years ago I read about a study done at some Ivy League school. They set up two rooms that had no furniture and four walls. The only thing one had was wallpaper with vertical stripes. The other room had only wallpaper with horizontal stripes. They took a group of eight kittens and placed four of them in each room. After a couple of months of growing in their environments, they took the cats from the room with the horizontal wallpaper and put them into a room full of furniture. Those cats kept bumping their heads into the vertical table legs. They could not see them or any other vertical item in the room and never could adapt. The opposite was true for the cats from the vertical wallpapered room. They could not see the flat surfaces, although they saw the table legs. This holds true in so many situations. Your power, if you choose to take it, is to set a good picture in the new customers mind when you first see them. If you do, they won't see the mistakes, (as the cats could not see the table legs), should you ever make one.

In my training approach, I also like to go over the definition of being a professional. I ask the person their definition first and I listen. I agree with everything they say and keep encouraging a larger definition. After that, I fill in if they leave anything out of my definition. A professional knows their products and services. They know how to do their jobs. They look good with clean clothes and grooming. All the definitions are great, but the point I try to make is that we all have highs and lows in life. Good days and bad days. When we are on a high and feel good about life, we all do a great job. There are times we are on a low regarding life. This is when a professional performs. They do a good job on their bad days as well as their good days. No one would ever know they had a bad day. They keep it to themselves.

Lastly in my training, I emphasize the golden rule. "Do onto others as you would have them do onto you." I emphasize this when we do dishes. Do them as if someone was washing

your dishes.

Review of chapter nine

In this chapter, we discussed:

* Giving new people an orientation.

* How to train to clean a rest room.

* How to know they know.

* What to do with a slow and thorough trainee.

* The way you start out a new person is the way they will always be.

* Set a good first impression.

* Vertical versus a horizontal world.

* How a professional acts.

CHAPTER TEN

Quality Service

Quality Service

In this chapter, we will discuss:

* Maintaining a quality service.

* Check! Check! Check!

* Giving a report on the job done.

* Checking the janitor form.

* Giving tickets for compliments.

* What prizes do I give?

* If all else fails, give a guarantee.

Quality

Quality is a word that is hard to understand. I don't believe it can be defined, because quality means different things to everyone you do business with. That is why I try to find the issues of importance of each customer I do business with. Dusting could be an issue for one customer. Rest room cleaning could be for another. You have got to find the issues for each client. This will let you satisfy that person. Assuming that you know the customer's most important issues, train the janitor this at that location first and check.

Check, check, check. This is the best way to deal with quality. When you have a new janitor that cleans alone, they must be checked. Some dirt does not show up for a month. For example, edges of carpets. When you are initially training, the edges are clean and unless you check, these type of problems show up later. After a ninety day period, when your janitor is consistent, you won't have to check them that often. You should check on a regular basis to be sure that quality is done.

When I first had janitors, I used to give report cards when I checked on their work. I did this because it was an easy way to give direction without having people upset with me. After a janitor has cleaned for two hours, the last thing they feel like doing is taking directions about everything they did wrong. More importantly, just criticizing a job does not reward and reinforce the aspects done right. I used to score as if someone was performing at the Olympics. I would give scores of 9.5 to 9.9. If someone was so bad to be below 9.5, I wouldn't keep them. I bragged how I never gave out a perfect "10."

When I did check, the first area to fill out was the, "what was done right," and then "areas to make adjustments." I listed as much as I could done right, as long as it was sincere. Whatever

you sincerely compliment will reinforce that action in your

janitor. Compliment a great dusting job and you will create a

janitor that is a great duster. Never give a phony compliment.

You will lose your credibility. I would say, "great dusting on that

desk, I like the way you made sure the chairs, magazines and

tables are straight…etc." Then I gave a score. The whole thing

became a game as everyone tried to get a perfect "10."

Checking the janitor form

Items done right:

Areas to make adjustments:

Score:

I did have to give someone a perfect "10" once. I had a person named Maria who cleaned a beauty salon. When I checked her work it was perfect. As I was checking, she explained a dilemma she had. She just got through waxing the floor, was at the front door when she realized that one of the beauty salon chairs was turned off to the left. It was not positioned straight to the mirror in front. She knew that would knock off her score. She swung herself on the top of the front door to a window seat behind the door. She then jumped from the window seat to the first salon chair, then to the next salon chair and from there, straightened the off centered chair. Then jumped back, straightened that one, then jumped back straightened that one, then jumped to the window seat, straightened that one and finally swung back on the top of the door to the building entrance. I never thought I would give a "10," especially not in a beauty salon, with the hair, hairspray on the mirrors, and other assorted problems associated with cleaning these type places. It was an incredible job. Why did she do it? She was a professional (and I had a good eye in recruiting), but those challenges to get a "10" worked over and over. It took a process that was a hassle to do and made it a fun game.

Another story of the report cards is with a former part time college student I hired named Mark. Mark never got a "10." I only gave one out in my life. He was highly motivated to do a great job and got high scores. He had a summer job with me and in September his parents wanted him to quit. His father owned a large company and was willing to pay Mark the same amount he made from me if he would quit working and concentrate on school. Let me ask you, would you rather clean offices or get paid to not clean offices? Mark chose to clean. Mark's father had to interview me to understand why his son would do this when he had trouble motivating, not only his son, but many of his own employees. I told his father that besides making a game of the work, I kept praising his son. I listened to what his dreams were and encouraged him. Mark wanted to play the drums and up until now his father was against it. They never communicated anymore. As a result of our talk, the father had a sound proof room built in the basement of their home. I brought a father and son together. Then to my surprise, I also lost my employee. Mark quit, went to school and got paid to play the drums in his new room. One great thing did happen to me from this. The father was so impressed, he hired my cleaning company to clean his 12,000 square foot office. Not only did I get this account, after I gave my estimate to clean it, he raised it by a couple hundred dollars a month. He thought I charged too little.

What I really did in both cases was praise people. I make an effort to notice what people did well. We all want someone to notice what was done. Sometimes I used to wish someone would see me on a spy camera doing a great job. Even though I was the owner, I wanted and needed praise. We all need the same things.

Another thing that I did to improve quality was to give tickets like the ones at arcades. The more tickets you collect or earn, the bigger prize you can turn them in for. I gave "A," "B," and "C." tickets for feedback from customers. If a customer called or sent in a postcard with a quality rating on it, I would give tickets.

A "C" compliment was for doing your job. For example, if a customer calls and says the janitor did a "great job," The janitor gets 1 ticket.

A "B" compliment is doing more than your job calls for and the janitor gets 3 tickets. For example, I had a customer call and thank the janitor for placing a case of Coke in the refrigerator.

An "<u>A</u>" compliment was going way beyond the job. For example, I got a call from a tenant in a large office complex we cleaned who said they got a call from one of their patients. The tenant was a doctor. Their patient called. When she left from her appointment with the doctor, her ride never showed up. She was in pain and crying. My janitor asked the problem and gave the woman a ride home. The woman thought this was the greatest thing anyone could have done and called the doctor. Obviously the tenant was happy and told me and the property manager. How could I not consider this an "A" type compliment? This got 10 tickets plus mention in the "book of honor" that listed all of the highest honors that have been accomplished in the history of my company.

When a person came to work at my company, I would ask what type of prizes they would like that they would never spend money on, because it was not a priority like rent or food.

I would purchase those items with the amount of tickets needed to get it. For example, one person who worked for me loved the Minnesota Vikings. I purchased a Vikings helmet signed by Randy Moss. Another of my employees loved the Chicago Bulls. I purchased an autographed picture of Michael Jordon. I used incentives to achieve the quality I sought, but incentives alone will not train people properly on how to clean. Incentives only make working fun. Let's review. Quality begins with defining the niche of worker that best fits your situation. Add proper training of telling, showing and then checking. Quality and your service can be enhanced through rewarding people when they do actions that you want.

Finally, should your service breakdown for any reason, offer a guarantee, a no-question guarantee. I had a customer that used my carpet cleaning service for his home carpets. Three months after the service, that customer called with a complaint.

He said he did not like the way the carpets came out. I asked why he waited three months to tell us. I tell customers they have 24 hours to notify us although if they called a year later I would honor a guarantee depending on the circumstances. The man said he was out of the country for a month had meant to call, but had other things on his mind. I said, no problem and went right out to re-do his carpets.

He was so happy that I redid his carpets that he asked me to come to his office because he wanted to meet me. I got to his office, he was a tenant in a 50,000 square foot building. He was the largest tenant. He said he was very impressed with our guarantee. He asked me if I would like to clean that building. He called the property manager while I was sitting there. He told the property manager that he wanted my company to do the cleaning. He set an appointment and that was the easiest commercial bid I ever went on. I got the account. No one likes to lose money on a particular job because of a guarantee, but sometimes, you can

turn a negative into a positive.

Review for chapter ten

In this chapter, we discussed:

* Maintaining a quality service.

* Checking! Checking! Checking!

* Giving a report on the job done.

* Checking the janitor form.

* Giving tickets for compliments.

* Deciding what prizes do I give?

* If all else fails, give a guarantee.

Ron Piscatelli

Jump notes

CHAPTER ELEVEN

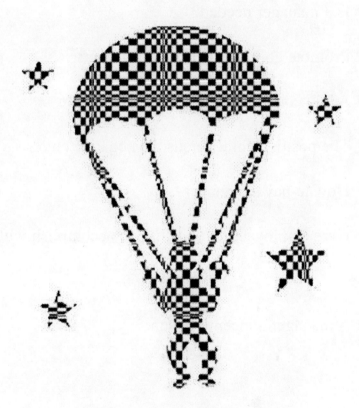

Hiring Managers

Hiring Managers

In this chapter, we will discuss:

* Is a manager needed?

* Promote good teachers.

* Avoid complainers.

* The positive child versus the negative child.

* How to pay a manager.

* Give employees an objective to accomplish with a time deadline.

* A manager's incentive plan.

Managers

With the simple plan of this book, a manager is not needed. You can do this yourself to save over-head costs. If you do hire a manager, they should work as a janitor at each location they manage. You can check at a location just cleaned by the janitor, but unless you know the place and nooks and crannies, items could easily be missed. I promoted part time managers from our janitorial staff.

I never liked the word manager. In my mind, I picture a king when I say manager. I see a person manipulating people's lives. I prefer to use the word responsible. As a person responsible for the accounts you assign to them, what they do is make sure the customer's needs are met. They are being responsible for the outcome. It is as simple as that. I have found that you can not force people to do things. You have to lead. You need to tell, show and check their work. Using the words "responsible for the outcome," will paint a picture in your manager's mind that his job is simple. Check that the job was done right.

Over the years, I have had many managers. I look for people who can teach. Just because a janitor is a good cleaner does not make him a manager. A good teacher can talk to people. I had a manager once who was a terrible teacher. No matter how many new recruits I sent him, the janitor stunk. None could clean well. I had another manager who could train any recruit to do a great job. Never a complaint from the manager. Both of these managers were excellent cleaners, yet one could teach and the other couldn't. Before you ever promote someone to manager, have them teach a new worker to see if they can do it. As you become experienced with promoting, your bench mark for quality management will change. Once you experience someone who can train anyone, you know that this is the prototype of manager you want. Don't settle for less.

I like my managers to be optimistic about the job and what has to get done. When you work with people, you can learn many things about how they think. Hire people who don't complain, even under the worst conditions. There was a story I heard years ago about an optimistic, positive little boy and a pessimistic, negative little boy. They did a study. They took the negative boy and placed him in a room full of every toy imaginable, a train and fire engine, etc... They told the little boy to play. They would come back in 15 to 30 minutes to see how he was doing. They took the positive boy and placed him in a room with horse manure. They would be back in 15 to 30 minutes later. When they got back to the room with the negative boy, he was crying. They said, "What's wrong? You have every toy to play with." The negative boy said that the train wasn't the right one. He said the fire engine was too small. He complained about everything. They went to see the other boy in the room of horse manure. The optimistic boy was laughing and throwing the manure up in the air. The instructor couldn't believe how happy he seemed to be and asked him why he was acting this way. The boy replied, "with all of this manure, there must be a pony somewhere!" The point is, you can not make a happy person out of a complainer. They will complain about everything. The manager that I talked about who never liked any of the janitors was always complaining when he was a janitor. He complained that the customers were dirty. If everything was clean he complained about something else. One time he complained about ants in the trash can. My feeling was, "who cares about those ants, just throw the trash away." The trash can he was talking about was the dumpster outside. I made a mistake by making him a manager and that's how you learn. How can a janitor complain about cleaning unless they are not right for the job? Cleaning is our job, not a chore. Think of it, if customers were clean they wouldn't need us. I am thankful when I see things dirty. It means I am needed. The last thing I want to hear is someone complain about dirt.

I get asked how to pay a manager. I used to pay a percentage of the gross at that account, usually 5% to 10%. When I added accounts, this gave the manager a raise. Should we lose an account, I could deduct that percentage off the manager's pay. If they covered a job when a janitor was out sick, I would pay that hourly amount to the manager. Even with all of those janitors, most of my managers were part timers. When I cut back from 75 janitors and 10 managers, I realized that it was easier and less expensive to just pay a manager a hourly wage should I need one for a particular large account. I paid them for what they did and I now call them an assistant for that job only with a list of responsibilities to accomplish. No titles. Even my managers were part time. They really did not need a title. Just a job description.

When I was working at various jobs in my younger days, I had bosses that would say to look busy. I hate this approach. I can look busy all day and never get things done. I loved bosses who would tell me what my job was and a deadline. There really are not many of them out there. It is you that has to initiate this approach. I learned this by accident. I was working at an alarm company that had a secretary named Mary. Mary worked for the owner of the company. She worked for the sales manager, the installing department manager and me, the office manager. She had four bosses. She answered phones, typed, filed, and did alarm signals. All day she complained about how much work she had to do. At five o' clock, the salesman, the alarm installers and all the other workers would file in the office before leaving for the day. We would all laugh and joke about things that happened. Mary would be working at her desk in front of us, until six to seven PM. She worked about ten hours a week overtime. We felt bad like we burdened her.

At Christmas we all chipped in to buy her a large color TV to thank her. A few months later she got a job for double what we were paying her. I hired a woman named Judy. I knew Judy would never finish because of my experience with Mary so I wrote out a list of her responsibilities. I said that if you finish early, you can relax. She did not have to look busy. Inside I was laughing because I knew she would not finish. I was hoping to cut back a little on those two extra hours a day.

My desk was situated where I could see Judy. After a few days, at ten AM, I saw Judy sitting there smoking a cigarette with her legs crossed doing nothing other than answer the phones. For a few days this kept repeating. I was concerned. Finally I said, "Judy, did you do all you could for the owner, sales manager, and alarm manager?" She said yes. I went over all of her responsibilities and they were done. She even found a huge stack of items to be filed that the previous secretary must have hid. I realized that besides answering the phones, our secretarial work took no more than two hours a day. By giving Judy her responsibilities with the incentive to do nothing when they were done, she got those items done in the first two hours of the day.

Mary, the former worker, complained all day, then did those two hours work as over time pay. If I hear someone complain, I now know it is because they are trying to convince me they are important, and get something done. I also know that they are the worst type workers you can hire. Don't confuse complaining with legitimate problems that need solutions. If someone does have an issue, I like them to bring a solution. A problem brought to you with a solution is not a complaint. The point is to promote janitors to managers who can teach, are optimistic, don't complain and offer solutions to improve things.

Today, no matter the project, I look for results. When you think this way, you have many options for incentives. One of the programs, I was most proud of, was the part time manager, 26 weeks a year paid vacation program. It almost seems impossible to give 26 weeks a year paid vacation. I teamed managers together. Once each manager had their routes of responsibility under control, one manager was on duty, the other off and they switched every other week. I could care less if they lived their lives and enjoyed themselves. The stipulations were that they had no complaints from any of their customers and they never took more than one week off at a time. Amazingly, managers would take a day off here and there. They never took 26 weeks. It gave them the freedom, almost as if they were self employed.

During this period, I had very few customer complaints, plus the

managers worked hard to have perfect scores.

Review of chapter eleven

In this chapter, we discussed:

* Whether to hire a manager.

* Promoting good teachers.

* Avoiding complainers.

* The positive child versus the negative child.

* How to pay a manager.

* Giving employees an objective to accomplish.

* A manager's incentive plan.

Ron Piscatelli

Jump notes

CHATER TWELVE

Incentives

Incentives

In this chapter, we will discuss:

* How to motivate people.

* A little white kitten as a business mentor.

* Janitor incentive number one.

* Janitor incentive number two.

* Janitor incentive number three.

* The janitor pool.

* The manager's incentive.

Incentives

Incentives can get anyone to do almost anything you want them to do. Why? Because people do things for their reasons, not your reasons. When I first got into the service business, my personal vision was to be the world's utmost authority on how to motivate people. After reading books, listening to motivational tapes and studying successful people, I realized that there is no way to motivate people. People have to motivate themselves. What I did learn was that if I could find what people want, showed them how to get it by doing what I needed done, they would self motivate themselves to take actions.

One of my greatest mentors was a stray white kitten that used to come to my front door many years ago when I lived in an apartment. There were about 30 other units in the building.

215

The kitten was so cute. I gave it food and the kitten hung around. Everyone in the complex was feeding it. Cats are smart. They go to where the food and living conditions are the best. I laugh when I see signs that say lost cat. Cats don't get lost. If you don't treat them right, they move on. My little kitten stopped coming to my door. I wanted the cat so I went out and purchased people food, cans of tuna and chunks of chicken. The results were that I now had the cat coming to my door again. I realized that working with employees has the same results. If you want the best, you have to provide the best pay compared to your competition.

With the janitors, I knew there were certain things I wanted them to do.

1.) Wear a uniform and hat

2.) Wear their ID badge

3.) Never call in sick

4.) Never get a complaint

5.)   Get compliments

These were the main things. If you have a great janitor that forgets to wear a hat, what do you do, yell at him? He will quit if you do that. Why make a great worker quit over a hat or ID badge? The main goal is doing a good job. I got an idea for incentives. I started this back in 1982 when the minimum wage was $3.50 per hour. I started the janitors at $3.50 per hour.

Incentive #1:

To get $4.00 per hour, the employee had to be sure their file was complete (Bring in a picture for an ID badge, finger prints and all of their paper work done). It was up to them to get them in.

Incentive #2:

Each month, a janitor only got $4.00 per hour as their base pay. They could get up to $2 more per hour right away for that month only by wearing their uniform, hat, ID badge, had perfect attendance, and no complaints. You may think that an employee should do this anyway. They should, but they don't. Again, if the janitor is a great cleaner, why be in a position to be a boss and force your will on them? This only creates resentment. You can win the battle, but if people quit, you are always hiring and training.

Incentive #3:

If a customer calls in or sends a postcard that we leave at their location with a compliment, the janitor is eligible for a monthly pool of money. I figured that I was willing to pay $6.00 per hour to the janitor, (today in 2004, it is $8 to $10 per hour). If someone didn't wear their uniform, they would not get the $2 per hour bonus that month. That extra $2.00 per hour would go into a pool of money. If you have 100 part time worker's working ten hours each per week, it comes out to 1,000 man hours a week. In four weeks that comes to 4000 man hours a month. That $2 per hour would go into the pool. If 99 of those 100 people did not qualify because of not wearing a uniform, that would come out to $2 times 4000 man hours or $8,000.

Let's say only one person did the things necessary to qualify for the pool, they would get the whole $8,000 bonus for that month. If ten people qualified, they would equally split the pool.

Most of the time, everyone qualified for $2 extra per hour and received $6 per hour, the amount I was going to pay them anyway. Pool totals were never higher than $100.00 to $200.00. Knowing it could happen was enough to motivate the staff. I never had to waste time telling people what to do. They did it for their reasons. They worked to get compliments to qualify for the pool. I also gave tickets for prizes for compliments.

Incentives will work for every situation. Just decide the outcome you are looking for. Let's take America's need for oil. Why not give incentives to investors to invest in alternative fuel sources? Let's say if you invest in an alternative fuel source company, you get to deduct that amount directly from your taxes. That alone would give a person, investing, nothing to lose and it would give these companies working capital to develop the alternative fuel. Then, should the company invent a process for fuel where we no longer will need foreign oil, that would mean that those people who invested would make big money. Next, have an incentive for absolutely no capital gains taxes on that income. This would create millions of companies competing to create that alternative fuel source with investors everywhere. It would not be long before someone comes up with something that is effective. Where would terrorists nations get money if you took oil revenues away? Once the fuel source was invented, the tax investing – incentive program would end. Think of a problem and there is an incentive that can produce effective results. Why has no one either thought of that solution or implemented that strategy? Oil was cost effective up until now and no one realized that oil revenues were paying terrorists. Fortunately for you in your business, you are the boss. You are the one in charge. You can break away from how everyone else does it and make getting the job done fun for your employees.

Managers had incentives to take 26 weeks off a year as long as they got no complaints. I never had to be a boss. I just had to be creative and be able to communicate those ideas to the staff.

All incentives are based on getting effective results. It didn't matter if a person was white or black, Catholic or Jew, gay or straight or male or female. Results and bonuses were based on performance. I have my favorites who work for me. Usually people who treat you well and follow everything you say become

favorites. We all have favorites, but bonuses were paid based on

performance, and thus fair for all.

Review of chapter twelve

In this chapter, we discussed:

* How to motivate people.

* How a little white kitten was a business mentor.

* Janitor incentive number one.

* Janitor incentive number two.

* Janitor incentive number three.

* The janitor pool.

* The manager's incentive.

Ron Piscatelli

CHAPTER THIRTEEN

Kobayashi Maru

Ron Piscatelli

Kobayashi Maru

In this chapter, we will discuss:

* Getting employees to want to improve performance.

* The Kobayashi Maru test.

* Captain Kirk and Star Trek

* The official scoring sheet rules.

* The office portion.

* The rest room portion.

* The lobby.

* The corridor.

* The scoring sheet and what is judged.

Kobayashi Maru

Most janitors work hard at the locations they are assigned to. My theory is anyone can clean a dirty place. When you are done, the customer can see a difference. Plus, a customer that allows a place to get dirty beyond the normal level, has no need for perfection. A clean place is very common, especially in professional suites in large commercial buildings. These type customers want to see a difference when they come in to work. These type of customers notice every fingerprint. When a janitor cleans, even if checked by a manager, very minor things can be missed. That is why the cleaning test, the "Kobayashi Maru" was established. It focuses on all of the little things that easily can be missed. Plus, it put "fun" into the training. It became a game instead of a boring lecture of what to do. Being a game, it got the workers in the habit of looking out for the little things. It got employees to think about ways to be more efficient which was rewarded with points. The person with the highest total score wins a designated prize, (see the official scoring sheet at the end of this chapter), dinner out for two at a nice restaurant or a new TV set. Make the prize desirous.

The Kobayashi Maru, named by the old T.V. series, Star Trek, is a leadership test given to potential star ship Captains, on how they would react under a "no win" scenario. In the show, the point was to find leaders that displayed great character in difficult situations.

At my company, the cleaning skills test called the Kobayashi Maru, is a fifty five points leadership test. Our whole service is based upon the fifty five items tested. In a way, we are in a no win situation with the customers. After we clean, we wipe away the evidence. The customer is looking for what we missed instead of what we did. This test will address those issues.

In the actual Star Trek episode, regarding the Kobayashi Maru test, it was revealed that Captain Kirk was the only person to ever pass the test. It came out that he rigged the test so he could win. Some would say this is cheating. Starfleet command cited Kirk for his ingenuity.

Hopefully we can rig the end scores when it comes to serving the customer on a <u>consistent</u> basis. We can turn what could be looked upon as a no win situation and make it a big win situation. Not only for the customer, but for all of us. Not only will the customer cite us for our ingenuity, but our income level will grow as a result!

Official Scoring

25 Points………………the fastest time

5 Points each………..route sheet items(2)

1-10 Points each………introduce a innovative cleaning tool (new item once reported to GM will be counted at next games so as to put in use inventions as they come up to be shared)

1-10 Points each………………introduce an innovation in cleaning

1 Point each…………………………..each point(55) on Kobayashi Maru

Deductions

1/5 Point deduction…..for each chair out of place (other than the one being tested)

…...for each paper on floor…

…..for each paper on a desk not straight…

…..for each picture frame not straight

…..for any item that takes away from an overall neat and orderly appearance

The following lists are the items that I tested. You can have a test on anything you choose. If you get complaints from customers, these would be great items to place on the test. I usually started with our office cleaned to perfection. Then I would set a trap on each item on the list and hide it as best as possible. The person tested had to search. The test and the traps were the same for each person. They couldn't finish until they found each item-trap on these lists.

Office/Suite Portion

1) Go over <u>Route Sheet</u>, 2 pet peeves (the duties of an account)

2) Magazines orderly

3) Trash can straight & how to tie a trash can liner

4) Desk literature trays. Dust ledges & insides

5) Coffee rings on a desk

6) Under desks, get on knees & brush out

7) Close drawers on desks if left open

8) Dust blinds and dust sills

9) Blinds are to be left in the same position

10) Pictures on the walls, straighten

11) Brush down upholstery

12) Brush down chair mat

13) Straighten items on the desk

14) Check behind doors

15) Fingerprints on doors

16) Check light switches for prints

17) Properly dressed with feather duster/brush/bags/ sponge/ paper towels

18) Uniform tucked in, cleaned and pressed

19) Hat

20) Wearing your I.D. badge

21) Key ring with the building key on the ring

22) Apron

23) Wipe sides of trash cans for spills

24) Inside glass partitions, clean & spot

25) Chairs straight around tables, desks, in front of desks, sides of magazine table

26) Microwave/coffee area/glass table for spots

27) Stainless sink in suite

28) Lines in carpet- light night

29) Vacuum carpet- heavy night

Rest room portion

30) Soap filled & tested

31) Paper towels & tested

32) Toilet paper

33) Seat covers

34) Fold toilet paper

35) Strip on the toilet seat

36) Sit on toilet seat and see customer perspective

37) Base of toilet

38) Hinge area under seat of toilet

39) Mirror clean top to bottom

40) Men's urinal, drips in front of bowl & floor

Lobby Portion

41) Entry mats vacuumed

42) Spills on floor

43) Stainless steel on elevators

44) Elevator tracks

45) Lines on carpet in elevators

46) Edges of carpet in elevators

47) Dust sills

Corridor Portion

48) Door prints

49) Ceiling vents dusted

50) Janitor left to right- doors locked

51) Janitor left to right- check stairwell

52) Manager left to right-check supplies-towels/soap

dispenser works

53) Manager left to right- check supplies-toilet paper/

seat covers

54) Manager left to right- door locked

55) Manager notice overall appearance

The following sheets were used to score the employees

that took the test.

Make a sheet for each participant. Give a possible point on each.

Office Suite Portion   Item/trap

1.) Proper Supply kit & tools inc. restroom   1

2.) Uniform clean, pressed and tucked in   1

3.) Hat   1

4.) ID   1

5.) Key ring w/only master   1

6.) Apron   1

7.) Dressed w/feather duster, brush, bags, sponge.   1

START TIME

8.) Spray Endust on feather duster over bucket   1

9.) Go over route sheet   1

10.) Turn off alarm   1

11.) Check customer log book and page in   1

12.) Clean in left to right direction

1

13.) Trash cans straight/tie a liner   1

14.) Desk literature trays/dust ledges & inside   1

15.) Coffee rings on desk   1

16.) Under desk on knees & brush out   1

17.) Close drawers on desk if left open   1

18.) Magazines orderly   1

19.) Dust items on desk, stapler/computer/calculator   1

20.) Dust blinds & sills   1

21.) Wash phone, mouthpiece & well   1

22.) Blinds left in same position   1

23.) Dust bottoms of chairs   1

24.) Pictures on wall, dust & straighten   1

25.) Brush down upholstery   1

26.) While cleaning, customer asks janitor to do task   1

27.) Janitor adds request to route sheet for manager   1

28.) Straighten items on desk   1

29.)Accuses janitor not getting clean item asked prior 1

30.) Check behind doors   1

31.) Fingerprints on doors   1

32.) Fingerprints on molding around door   1

33.) Light switches for prints   1

34.) Wipe sides of trash cans for spills   1

35.) Chairs straight around conference table   1

36.) Inside glass partitions, clean & spots   1

37.) Chairs straight in front of desks

1

38.) Microwave/coffee area/glass table for spots/print   1

39.) Stainless steel sink in suite   1

40.) Lines in carpet light night   1

41.) Vacuum carpet heavy night   1

42.) Turn around notice overall appearance   1

43.) Set alarm   1

44.) Single door turn around method w/shake rattle & roll

1

45.) Route sheet item   5

46.) Route sheet item   5

Total

Total   54

Overall Appearance 1-10 PTS   10

Going for an "A" Compliment   10

Happy Attitude/Enthused/Smile   10

Ron Piscatelli

Office Deductions	<1/5>
Notice Something No One Else	10
Introduce Innovative Tool	10
Introduce Innovative Technique	10
TOTAL BACK PAGE	60
Time 1st Pass	
Time 2nd Pass	Best Time
Time 3rd Pass	25 pts below
Time 4th Pass	

FINAL TIME

You can keep score any way that works for the end result you are seeking. I gave points on the items that I felt were important to provide a great service. I got the janitors and managers to think of those cleaning issues as basics. This is the way we clean. It was natural. Work should be fun even if it is janitorial. Why not put fun into the job? As the owner, it is up to you.

Review of chapter thirteen

In this chapter, we discussed:

* Getting employees to want to improve performance.

* The Kobayashi Maru test.

* Captain Kirk and Star Trek

* The official scoring sheet rules.

* The office portion.

* The rest room portion.

* The lobby.

* The corridor.

* The scoring sheet and what is judged.

Ron Piscatelli

CHAPTER FOURTEEN

Three Biggest Sins

Three biggest sins

In this chapter, we will discuss:

* What is a sin?

* What is a mortal sin?

* What is a cleaning sin?

* Leaving a door unlocked.

* Not setting an alarm system or setting one off.

* Forgetting to replenish rest room supplies, especially toilet paper.

Three Biggest Sins

In the janitorial business, there are many things that can go wrong. Some are more serious than others. I think of it as committing sins.

Being brought up Catholic, I remember the nuns in Sunday school emphasizing the differences between committing a sin and a mortal sin. A sin that was not one of the Ten Commandments was a minor infraction. If you died before confession, meant a time in purgatory. You would end up in heaven eventually. A mortal sin would land you in hell for eternity if you died before confession. Obviously, it was wise to know the difference if your goal was heaven.

In cleaning, you have errors that are minor and ones that are major or mortal. If you make a cleaning error, you will probably be told and given the opportunity to correct it. Customers will cancel if they have to tell you over and over the same problem. In this chapter, I will talk about the three mortal sins of janitorial. Should you or one of your people commit one, you could lose the account quicker than you can imagine even if they love you. The three are:

#1: leaving a customer's door unlocked,

#2: either not setting the alarm or a false alarm sent in and

#3: forgetting the supplies in the rest room especially toilet paper.

Trust can dissipate very quickly if you leave a customer's door unlocked when you leave. Customers have concerns giving out a key to their business. There is no excuse for forgetting to lock a door. The first thing to solving every problem is to get to the root of the problem. The problem is believing our minds are capable of memory. As a former poor speller, I was always made to feel unworthy of life during spelling bees in school. You are asked to spell a word. If you misspell, you disappoint your teammates and you are humiliated by being forced to sit. What a waste of time. When I was studying the Italian language, I realized that Italian words are spelled as they are said. Each sound is consistent with its letter. In English, there are more sounds than letters in the alphabet. For example the "A" sound in cat and care are different. Also, the same sound can be used by more than one letter. For example, the "F" and "Ph" are the same as in the word for and phone. What a waste of time and of the use of our brains.

What does this have to do with locking doors? Everything! It starts with memory. Our brains do not memorize, they associate. Our minds move from subject to subject through triggers that spark an association to things. If I say coffee, you might think

Starbucks. Someone else may think Maxwell House. Someone else may think of being unhealthy. Everyone may have different associations, but associations trigger thoughts or actions. By understanding this fact, you can solve the problem of leaving any door unlocked by creating a pre-planned trigger so janitors will not have to rely on their memories.

When a person cleans a place over and over, it becomes a routine. It is easy to think of a million other things when you clean. I can not tell you how many times I would be on my way to another location when I would think, "did I lock that door?" I'd drive all the way back to check. I had to come up with a way to remind me to check when I was locking the door. I came up with a title I called the "hokey-pokey." After I closed the customer's door, I would do that dance where you turned yourself around and then I would double check the door. I must have looked crazy being alone turning and dancing, but I knew that door was locked. I trained every janitor the same way. This was the trigger to lock doors.

Another way I titled a trigger was with the "shake, rattle, and roll" method of locking doors. Even if a door is locked, it may not be pushed all the way into the door jam. By shaking the handle, rattling the handle and finally rolling the handle in and out of each door, prevented this problem from happening. If a location had many locked doors the janitor would do a walk around going left to right to check each door. This trigger appropriately was titled the "left to right method." When I trained my new janitors, they saw me do this. I was consistent. If you don't set the example, no one will follow this procedure. Since I instituted this procedure, I never had a door left unlocked.

False alarms were solved by teaching janitors how to use the alarm. I used to manage an alarm company in San Diego. I noticed that people who just got a new alarm system would have a false alarm when they first used their system. As I studied

the alarm installers, I realized they told people how to use their

system, but never really showed them. Therefore, when I showed

a person how to do their alarm, I would show. Then, I had them

do it. We set the alarm and went outside. I put shopping bags in

their hands as if they were coming home. Isn't this how they will

come home? No one made errors after this training. If they did,

I was there to correct the problem. I did the same with janitors

except instead of shopping bags, they had cleaning tools in their

hands. When they went into the location, they had to find the

lights and the alarm key paid. I showed them how to call the

alarm company and abort a false alarm in case they set one. I had

them role play talking to the alarm operator.

To be sure we set the alarm I had janitors leave their car

keys on the floor under the alarm. The customer's keys as a rule,

stay connected to the janitor's body. That way the janitor would not lock themselves out. When the janitor picks up his car keys off the floor, this served as a trigger to set the alarm. All of these procedures became habits that triggered the actions that needed remembering.

The last of the three biggest sins was not placing toilet paper in the rest room. I could not think of a trigger for this except that the first thing you do in a rest room is replenish the supplies. I found that if a janitor needed to go get a supply, but cleaned first, they could forget to come back with the supply. No one wants to stop cleaning to run back to the supply room for something. Again, don't rely on memory! There is no such thing. Get in the habit of doing supplies first and you won't have to rely on your memory.

One last thing on memory, I went to college to be a history teacher. My father as a joke, would ask me, "When was the war of 1812 fought?" I would say, "Dad, I don't know and I don't care." He would say, "what kind of a history teacher are you?"

I said, "If I want the answer, I can look in a reference book. My mind was meant to solve problems by being open to answers when they come to me." If my mind is filled with facts or trying to remember things, then it won't be open to new ideas.

It is your choice what you want to use your mind for. As a leader, I'd rather use mine to solve any problem.

Review of chapter fourteen

In this chapter, we discussed:

* What a sin was.

* What a mortal sin was.

* What a cleaning sin was.

* Leaving a door unlocked.

* Not setting an alarm system or setting one off.

* Forgetting to replenish rest room supplies, especially toilet paper.

Ron Piscatelli

Jump notes

CHAPTER FIFTEEN

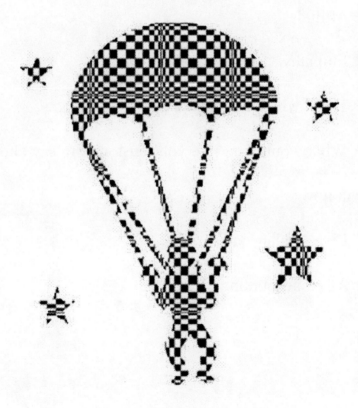

This and That

This and that

In this chapter, we will discuss:

* Attitude.

* Empathy.

* Think win, win, and win.

* What would you like your customer to say about you a year from now?

* Live a balanced life.

* A few accounting ideas.

This and That

Attitude makes the difference

Your attitude makes all the difference in everything you do. You get back what you put out. Put out a storm and a storm is what you get back. Give out a smile and you get back a smile. Care about your customers and employees, and they will care about you.

Separate your sales and service departments. I made the mistake of teaming a salesman and a service manager. They ran off and stole a couple of customers to form their own business. Fortunately, my employees signed papers that allowed me to sue them for the stolen accounts. They settled out of court and paid me. However, I still lost a couple of customers and a great deal of mental thought. I realized I did not lose an account where I had established rapport with the manager or owner. Always develop rapport with your customers.

Develop empathy towards your customers and your employees. Empathy means placing yourself in someone else's shoes. Try to think of how others feel. Go inside their skin. This will give you great insights on how to treat people.

Always think, "Win, win and win." In all of your dealings, be sure your customers win with quality service. Be sure your employees win with their pay and working conditions. Finally, be sure you win because you are in business to make a profit. Don't be ashamed to want to make a profit. Know when to walk away from a potential new customer when it does not make you profit, does not fit your niche, or there is not good chemistry in the atmosphere.

A great exercise to improve your service to your customers is to pretend you are a year in the future. Your customer is talking to a reporter. What would you want that customer to say about you? Take a moment and dream now about what you would like them to say. List below all that you can think of.

_____

_____

_____

_____

_____

_____

_____

_____

_____

_____

_____

_____

_____

_____

_____

_____

Whatever you list as what you want the customer to say about you is how you should act every day towards your customers. You have a blueprint of what you need to do today so your customers will say that about you in the future.

Live a Balance Life

Life is not just about making money. There are many areas of your life that needs attention to have a full life. Some of the areas are:

1)Business/ Your Vocation

2)Family

3)Friends

4)Health/ Physical

5)Spiritual

6)Love

Be sure to have goals in each area and work on them daily. Think of a pie cut up into 6 sections. Each area needs work to have a full life. Don't give up your family to work 24 hours a day.

At death, no one regrets missing a business meeting, but they do regret missing their child growing up. While there were times I was frustrated with the janitorial business dealing with customers and employees, I was blessed that this business allowed me to be home with my family. I got to see my kids grow up.

Accounting

I am not going to say too much in regards to the accounting department other than it is one of the three most important areas of a business. The other two being your service and the marketing/sales areas. There are a couple of things I will recommend.

1) Get a computer and use Quickbooks for your program. Then learn this program. In the long run, you will be very organized and able to handle all of your accounting needs yourself should you choose to do it. (For Quickbooks seminars,

go to www.CoffeeBreakWisdom.com) There are payroll services out there if you rather someone else do it.

2) Get an accountant for your tax needs. Pay your taxes!

3) The thing with your billing is to get the bills out on the last day of the previous month you are invoicing for. If today is June first, your bill should be sent out yesterday for the month of June dated May 31st and date due by the 15th of June. Customers usually follow whatever policy you have. This gets your money in by the end of the month cleaned. Some pay as soon as they get the bill and you have a positive cash flow.

4) Do not give credit for more than the month being cleaned. If a customer can't pay one month, two won't be easier.

5) Buy all of your supplies from your supplier with a check. No credit should be used. Charging equipment and supplies will add up very quickly.

Ron Piscatelli

Accounting is not easy if you are not familiar with it, but once you learn what you need to do and have a professional accountant available for questions, it will become part of your life. Just seek advice from those in business that have no problems collecting. Collecting is easy when you stay on top of it. Only seek answers from people who are succeeding with little effort in a positive manner in what you are trying to accomplish.

Review of chapter fifteen

In this chapter, we discussed:

* Attitude.

* Empathy.

* Think win, win, and win.

* What would you like your customer to say about you a year from now?

* Live a balanced life.

* A few accounting ideas.

Ron Piscatelli

Jump notes

The

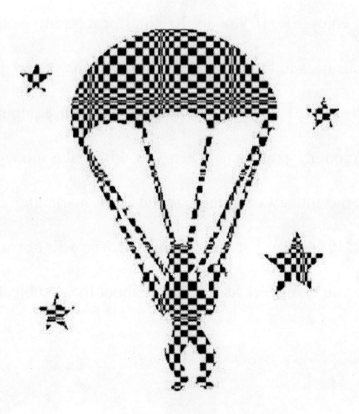

Conclusion

The Conclusion

The janitorial business has been great to me. It has allowed me to support my family for over 20 years. It has given me free time to enjoy life. If you are looking for a steady income, this is the business to be in, but a word of caution. <u>Keep it simple!</u> Keep over-head down. Don't buy trucks and equipment that create monthly payments. Then you will make money. If you ever spend money on things, spend it on marketing and sales courses. If you can not market and sell, you will not succeed. I believe you can never learn enough about those subjects. There is always business out there. There is no such thing as a bad

economy when you are in the janitorial business.

Good Luck,

Ron Piscatelli

P.S. I would love to know about your progress. Let me

know what you think of the information in this book.

Go to: www.JumpIntoJanitorial.com

Ron Piscatelli

Ron Piscatelli

Jump notes

Ron Piscatelli

Jump notes

Ron Piscatelli

Jump notes

Ron Piscatelli

Jump notes

If you would like to be notified

about

1)   free coaching teleconferences

and

2) articles to increase your

janitorial business,

Go to:

www.JumpIntoJanitorial.com

Then,

submit your name

and

e-mail address

for our

free newsletter.

If you would like information on

1) hiring a coach,

2) consulting services

or for

3) seminar information,

call or write to:

Ron Piscatelli

P.O. Box 34075

San Diego, California 92163

(619)294-7865

website:

www.JumpIntoJanitorial.com

* Call for a free half hour of coaching at

(619)294-7865

*(subject to availability)

About the Author

Ron Piscatelli is the author of the book, "Coffee Break Wisdom on Starting a Successful Business." This is a book on how to start and build a successful business netting over six figures per year. Visit that site at: www.CoffeeBreakWisdom.com

He is also the author of the book, "Pasta FaZool For The Soul." The Italian cookbook everyone is talking about.

Visit that site at: www.PastaFaZoolForTheSoul.com

He is the President of Global Building Services providing professional janitorial and cleaning services to the San Diego area, for over 23 years. Visit that site at: www.JanitorialSanDiego.com

He is President of Goal Achievers goal groups for entrepreneurs doing coaching, consulting, facilitating and brainstorming teleconferences.

He is married to wife Ellen and they have been together for over thirty years. They have two beautiful daughters, Pia and Alex. Ron is also an artist. See Ron's Art at: www.RonPiscatelli.com

Piscatelli

Quick order form

* Hard cover $34.50 Soft cover $22.95

Visit our website at:
www.JumpIntoJanitorial.com

Telephone orders: 800.251-7805

Mail order: *Please send_____book/s to:*

Name_____

Address_____

City:_____State:_____Zip_____

Phone:_____

E-mail address:_____

Sales tax: Please add 7.5% for orders shipped to California addresses.

Shipping and handling:
US $7.99

Payment: Credit card

__Visa __MasterCard

Card number:_____

Name on card:_____exp. date:_____

Signature:_____

Printed in the United States
48353LVS00008B/64-72